Aphrodite Rising
a Philosophy for Our Time

Aphrodite Rising
a Philosophy for Our Tima

Dick Sullivan

Coracle Books

By the same author:

Non-fiction
Old ships
Navvyman
Undertones: Mild Mysticism in an Age of Umber
Counter-Cosmos: the Mind of the Mystic

Fiction
Gideon's God

Poetry
Capperbar
Melanie
The Moon at Midnight
Morning on the Mountain

ISBN 978 0 906280 18 8

Sappho loved a world of whiteness,
Of moonlight white on Lydia
And on the sea, blanching
The white leaved woods of Lesbos.

But Sappho also loved the risen sun
And Aphrodite rising from the sea.

Contents

CHAPTER ONE: *Decline to Decline* 9

CHAPTER TWO: *Consciousness of Consciousness* 30

CHAPTER THREE: *The Making of the Modern Mind?* 37

CHAPTER FOUR: *The Concrete Cul-de-Sac* 44

CHAPTER FIVE: *Materialism and the Light of the Gods* 48

CHAPTER SIX: *The Uses of the Arts* 58

CHAPTER SEVEN: *Counter Consciousness* 68

CHAPTER EIGHT: *Immateriality Isn't Immaterial* 81

CHAPTER NINE: *A Pre-Plato Platonist* 92

CHAPTER TEN: *Reason Rising* 96

CHAPTER ELEVEN: *The Gothic IS Platonic* 110

CHAPTER TWELVE: *Applied Platonism* 117

CHAPTER THIRTEEN: *Berkeleyan Immaterialism* 127

CHAPTER FOURTEEN: *A Two-Legged West?* 135

Bibliography 148

Index 153

CHAPTER ONE

Decline to Decline

Is the West declining? The idea isn't new – Oswald Spengler's *The Decline of the West* came out in 1918. He was a schoolteacher born in 1880 in the Hartz Mountains and in some ways his book is what you'd expect from a thirty-five year old Victorian German. His main thesis is that Cultures are shaped by places, evolve into Civilisations and die at the end of a life span of roughly a thousand years. They are, literally, organisms: societies are like butterflies or orchids, coming and going without any plan or aim.

Cultures begin in folkways in the countryside and evolve over centuries into urbanised Civilisations dominated by a cult of money and Ibsen-ised women (or feminists) who no longer see motherhood as the purpose of life. *Cultures* are spiritual and at one with nature: *Civilisations* are intellectual and materialist. All end in dictatorships.

Western civilisation, Spengler thought, is based on space and a striving upwards to infinity – hence its Gothic cathedrals straining skywards with great windows leading out from holy interiors into the boundless. We have flying buttresses, flying machines, telescopes, perspective in painting, soaring music, physics: nor is it just upward, it's outward too – trekking to the icecaps, crossing oceans, climbing mountains. Now our thousand years of Culture-cum-Civilisation is up and it's time for us to go. His mistake was in not seeing the continuity between Homer and today: instead, he split us into the Greco-Roman and then, separately, into the modern West when, in fact, it's been Greek all the way: we've survived, with renewals, almost three Spenglerian life spans.

In 1918, also, Max Weber (1864-1920) said the West was

disappointed, disenchanted, with the world because of its over-reliance on rationality, having forgotten anything deeper or higher. Yet eighty years after Spengler and Weber, Jacques Barzun(1907-2012) was still saying the West was finished, giving his reasons in *From Dawn to Decadence,* published exactly at the turn of the Millennium. Society has fragmented into gridlock, log jam and stalemate, overwhelmed by diversity: people are for/against collectivism/individualism, high art/low art, irreligion/religion. Rights are bandied around and handed out indiscriminately to "illegal immigrants, children, criminals, babies, plants, animals." There is a longing for the primitive and the simple. At the same time, old art forms are worked out and institutions can no longer evolve. This civilisation is stale with nothing to offer but repetition, boredom, fatigue and an unhappy search for the spiritual – in Buddhism, TM, the Moonies, environmentalism, Global Warming, crystals and primal screams. This is a 'stalled society', filled with vitality and energy but deadlocked. New ideas are instantly opposed by contrarian groups, and all this amid a "floating hostility to things as they are". "The hope is that getting rid of what is, will by itself generate new life."

The subtitle of Allan Bloom's book, *The Closing of the American Mind* (1986) is: *How higher education has failed democracy and impoverished the souls of today's students.* The blurb carried on the theme: students in the 1980s were graduating with little learning, 'creativity' had replaced reason and scholarship: universities had been taken in by Continental ideas suitable only for failures: an understanding of Western history was a thing of the past and with it had gone any vision of the future, leaving graduates culturally destitute. Young Americans once went up to university with a background of religion they'd picked up as children, but no longer did. Rock music, which appealed barbarically to their raw and immature sexual longings, delved deep into their dark, primeval souls, and came up with Mick Jagger. But, of course, universities can't be blamed for those things, Jagger in particular: nor for the outlooks of new intakes of feminist and black students, neither of whom could accept that Western civilisation, all three thousand years of it, had been (on the whole) made by men who, because they were European, had also been (on the whole) white – as if differences in skin colour or genitalia could falsify thoughts and ideas.

Bloom also picked on the sexual revolution as being harmful because, when sex becomes 'no big deal', it debases life itself (Shakespeare's *Measure for Measure* goes into this more deeply). Divorce made young people over-self-protective, closing their minds to any philosophy or literature which could hurt them even more than life already had. He also highlighted the Germanification of America which started in the sociology departments of US universities in the late 1940s. These were ideas taken from Freud and Weber, who in turned took them from Nietzsche, rather than from Marx, although their American takers were either Marxists or left wing in some other way. They thought they were at the forefront of a second Scientific Revolution with themselves taking the parts of Galileo, Copernicus and Newton. In the event, they led the country into a kind of "nihilism without the abyss" because their nihilism was simply a 'vague disquiet' riding on an inner emptiness. Their students knew of Oedipus only through Freud, so ignorant were they of their own cultural inheritance.

A quarter of a century later things were worse. Theodore Dalrymple is the pen-name of Anthony Daniels, a medical doctor and psychiatrist who worked for several years in a slum hospital and city jail in the English West Midlands. His mother was a pre-War immigrant from Nazi Germany, a fact which gave her an outsider's view of England and which, in time, allowed her son to compare it with what England has become. Now, as he wrote in *Not with a Bang but a Whimper* (2009): "On practically all measures of social pathology, Britain leads the Western world, though only half a century ago it was better ordered, as well as freer, than most other societies." On the whole (and only on the whole), the pre-War English had been ironic, eccentric, self-deprecating, self-reliant, non-conformist, law abiding, taking the blame for their own wrong-doing, stoical, uncomplaining and tolerant. By the 21st century they'd become conformist, cowed, humourless, self-righteous, state-dependent, sentimental, self-pitying, intolerant of difference or dissent, dumb-downed, blaming everybody and everything except themselves for their failure and unhappiness (re-labelled 'depression' because it sounds more like a disease), violent, philistine, brutal abusive, trivial, feckless and semi-literate. Moral cowardice is rife in a country dominated by 'sociological secularists' to whom the lower classes are like "billiard balls, acted upon by forces that they cannot resist". The cause of this decline, this abject decay, is statism and Welfarism, the collectivist ideology of intellectuals, along with their doctrine of non-judgmentalism.

In *The Face of God* (2012) Roger Scruton gives another reason for the decline of the West, although without describing it as such: the loss of religion. "We should not be surprised, therefore, if God is so rarely encountered now. The consumer culture is without sacrifices; easy entertainment distracts from our metaphysical loneliness. The rearranging of the world as an object of appetite obscures its meaning as a gift. The defacing of *eros* and the loss of rites of passage eliminate the old conception of human life as an adventure within the community and an offering to others. It is inevitable, therefore, that moments of sacred awe should be rare among us." "By remaking human beings and their habitat as objects to consume rather than subjects to revere we invite the degradation of both." "Our disenchanted life is, to use the Socratic idiom, 'not a life for a human being.'

In the nearly hundred years between Spengler and Scruton others had their say, though few listened. Owen Barfield (1898-1997) wrote plays, poetry, novels and non-fiction – his best two books are *Poetic Diction* (1926), *Saving the Appearances* (1957). His theme was the evolution, and then the wreck, of Western consciousness. Until the scientific revolution of the 16th and 17th centuries, he argued, the Western mind was at one with nature, sharing or merging the consciousness of the individual with the all-pervading consciousness of the cosmos. To the people of those days the things of the world were alive with a kind of god-ness: the Medieval mind, he said, wore the cosmos like a garment, whereas we walk on it like a stage. We live isolated in minds walled in by the bone of the skull, looking out on a cosmos we no longer think of as a living thing as we stare out of our own darkness into a deadness of violent energy and hostile matter: as a result life for us is meaningless and the West is in trouble. Not that Barfield put much of it quite like that but it is, I think, a fair paraphrase.

Again, there was nothing too new about this. Although he wasn't talking about the decline of the West, G K Chesterton in his book *Orthodoxy* (1908) said something similar: the Transcendent is like the sun – a 'blaze and a blur': reason is like the moon – a cold Euclidean circle: by relying too much on reason, reason has reasoned itself into near extinction. "The poet only asks to get his head in the heavens. It is the logician who seeks to get the heavens into his head. And it is his head that splits." In 1901, in *The Defendant,* he also said: "The simple sense of wonder at the shape of things is the basis of spirituality" but the logical and over-rational can't see it.

Disaffection has been one outcome of all of this loss. Friedrich von Hayek's *The Road to Serfdom* was published in England early in 1944. He warned against totalitarianism in the West: Nazi Germany and Soviet Russia were just farther along the collectivist road and totalitarianism is wired into collectivisim. From 1870, the English concept of liberty stopped spreading across Europe and German socialism took its place. Very quickly, the English themselves became convinced that their ideas of liberty and free enterprise were selfish and that profits were wrong. German socialists were in the Bundestag in the late 19th century, years before the Labour Party was elected to Parliament. German socialism, said Hayek, was always an assault on the individualism which is at the very centre of the West and its success. (Kierkegaard (1813-1855), writing in the 1840s in Denmark, said something similar: only inwardness matters and it's being lost as individuals are re-absorbed into the pack – people were becoming copies of each other (though, he added, Christianity wants them to be individuals.)

Students returning to the UK and US from Germany and Russia in the 1930s, Hayek went on, were uncertain about whether they were Fascists or Communists – they hated the West, was all they knew. Why do intellectuals favour collectivism? Hayek asked. Because, Friedman replied, they're emotional, possibly more so than most non-intellectuals.

Nearly twenty years after Hayek's book, Kenneth Clark (1903-1983) fronted a television programme called *Civilisation.* Why do civilisations collapse? Clark gave several reasons. To begin with, they're fragile and can become so filled with fear – of war, disease, invaders, starvation – that people stop planning a future. Belief in the supernatural, too, Clark went on, can paralyse people by stopping the evolution of ideas. Loss of confidence can be a civilisation breaker, also. And tiredness, exhaustion, sapped energy: a kind of high entropy of listlessness. Civilisations also end through "greed and laziness" and because of the "unpredictable."

The danger for the future, Clark thought he foresaw, wasn't a lack of Yeatsian convictions (there are "rather too many of them") but in the loss of a centre. "The moral and intellectual failure of Marxism has left us with no alternative to heroic materialism, and that isn't enough. One may be optimistic, but one can't exactly be joyful at the prospect before us." A healthy West could, most probably, resist invasion and so, if it fails, it will be because it's been sapped from within. The sappers will be a mix of inner emptiness and a Fifth Column of the Left, both of the active and the passive kind.

Generalised loathing and particularised self-loathing are

two more results of this general collapse. Individuals have often hated themselves, of course – in the 1st century BC, for example, Lucretius wrote: "Each person tries to flee himself. Yet despite ourselves, we remain attached to this self which we hate." What is new is the scale of the hatred, which also seems to be wholly Western. Rightly or wrongly, Plotinus (204-270 AD), had an explanation: we have to choose between the higher (the spiritual) and the lower (matter) and, since nature requires us to rise, we feel self-contempt if we pick the lower over the higher, the bad over the good: to choose matter is to choose a dead end and so those who choose it are lessened and are therefore lesser.

In England, the Left's loathing of all things Western is often the loathing of all things English, and it isn't new. In Queen Anne's day Pope satirised people who praised every country but their own. Bishop Berkeley (not yet a bishop) wrote *Alciphron* in the early 1730s as a defence of Christianity against freethinking atheists. In one passage, Crito says: "If Mahometanism were established by Authority, I make no doubt, those very Free-thinkers, who at present applaud Turkish Maxims and Manners to that Degree you'd think them ready to turn Turks, would then be the first to exclaim against them." (Although his could be read as mere contrariness.)

Today's distaste, on the other hand, can also be traced back to the 1880s. William Morris, the millionaire (in today's money, that is) founder of the Arts and Crafts Movement, is a good character to start with. Asa Briggs said Morris hated the tastelessness of the middle classes, cared nothing for the institutions of his country, questioned its achievements, and scorned its values. He wasn't the last to do so: this particular mindset is now mainstream in much of England. George Orwell came up against all of this in the 1930s and '40s. The Left lumped millions of people into blocks labelled 'wholly good' or 'utterly bad'. The chosen group was idealised, even idolised: it could do no wrong, just as whoever opposed it could do no right. (You can see where he got the slogan: "four legs good, two legs bad".) The Utterly Bad was their own country, while the Wholly Good was Communism and the Soviet Union.

In the 1940s, socialists and communists annoyed Orwell most, particularly because of their Anglophobia in the middle of what was quite clearly a war to the death between the acceptable and the totally unacceptable. They didn't exactly want Hitler to win, just England to lose. British victories were disbelieved, British losses celebrated. Worse were the pacifists who not only hated democracy but admired totalitarianism. Their propaganda boiled down to saying one side was as bad as the other – except that England and the United States were worse. ("All animals are equal," perhaps, "but some are more equal than others.") To a pacifist, Churchill was the moral equivalent of Hitler. Russia wasn't blamed for fighting: Britain was.

Twenty or so years later, that minority (still a minority) was starting to get the upper hand and change the nature of England itself. Twenty or so years later, that minority (still a minority) was starting to get the upper hand and change the nature of England itself. It had a lot to work on. From my own experience I'd say that at the heart of many of the Post-War English was a cold emptiness filled with rage or, at their best, bad temper. It was as if something had died after the ending of the War. By the 1970s, patriotism had all but gone from middle class graduates, all of whom claimed to think for themselves yet curiously all thought the same thing: they'd ruin anybody who held a different opinion – that is, a non-left wing one. Peter Hitchens (a journalist and younger brother of the Christopher we'll meet in Chapter Seven) was a student in the 1960s. Back then he was both an atheist and a Trotskyist (later he gravitated to Anglicanism and the Tories). On 31st March, 2013, he wrote in his *Mail on Sunday* blog:

"When I was a Revolutionary Marxist, we were all in favour of as much immigration as possible. It wasn't because we liked immigrants, but because we didn't like Britain. We saw immigrants – from anywhere – as allies against the staid, settled, conservative society that our country still was at the end of the Sixties. Also, we liked to feel oh, so superior to the bewildered people – usually in the poorest parts of Britain – who found their neighbourhoods suddenly transformed into supposedly 'vibrant communities'. If they dared to express the mildest objections, we called them bigots."

"Revolutionary students didn't come from such 'vibrant' areas (we came, as far as I could tell, mostly from Surrey and the nicer parts of London). We might live in 'vibrant' places for a few (usually squalid) years, amid unmown lawns and overflowing dustbins. But we did so as irresponsible, childless transients – not as homeowners, or as parents of school-age children, or as old people hoping for a bit of serenity at the ends of their lives."

"When we graduated and began to earn serious money, we generally headed for expensive London enclaves and became extremely choosy about where our children went to school, a choice we happily denied the urban poor, the ones we sneered at as 'racists'. What did we know, or care, of the great silent revolution which even then was beginning to transform the lives of the British poor?   To us, it meant patriotism and tradition could always be derided as 'racist'."

"I have learned since what a spiteful, self-righteous, snobbish and arrogant person I was (and most of my revolutionary comrades were, too). I now believe that the unreasoning hatred comes almost entirely from the liberal Left. But, unlike me, most of the Sixties generation still hold the views I used to hold and they will not change.The screaming, spitting intolerance comes from a pampered elite who are ashamed of their own country, despise patriotism in others and feel none themselves. They long for a horrible borderless Utopia in which love of country has vanished, nannies are cheap and other people's wages are low."

What he didn't say is why? Why did the privileged classes hate their social inferiors so much that they were prepared to bring a whole country down in ruins, among which they would still have to live? What is the psychology behind all this? It would be easy to say it's the juvenility of the Boomers who can never grow up, except of course it pre-dates them. Orwell suggested it was the need to belong – a loss of both patriotism and faith left a vacancy, an emptiness, which had to be filled with something. He also noted that many of the people who shared this mindset in the 1930s and '40s were protected, like Morris, by private incomes. The present generation, as Hitchens acknowledges, earn 'serious money' and it's also been an age of unusual prosperity.

In the 1890s that way of thinking led Morris to a daydream of utopia. One result, his novel *News from Nowhere* (1890), could well be a blueprint for the green wing of socialism, foreshadowing as it does exactly what many of them seem to want – a machineless Medieval world but without its sickness, pain or squalor. Morris wrongly called his system communist: it is, more realistically, the Arts and Crafts Movement globalised (the whole world has followed London's example it seems). It's also an unrealisable fantasy of a world free of pain based on the false premise that you can change human nature by changing the nature of society. In 1955, soon after the revolution, the great clearance of houses began and London became an Edenic place of gardens, orchards, country houses, short streets of shops (everything is free: there is no money), and a wild wood.

This Nowhere is the fourteenth century with Victorian plumbing: the country of Edward III with a late nineteenth-century population living in hamlets in a greenwood. People are so happy it has made them all good looking (if not beautiful at least comely). No-one is unhealthy, all are long lived (are there any physicians?) There are no schools, no schooling, no police, soldiers, or government (apart from Mote Houses where purely local matters, such as replacing bridges, are voted on). Food is plentiful and free, even in restaurants and guest houses. Work, which is carried out only by those who want to, is based on the Arts and Crafts ethos – the industrial cities have been demolished. You have to ask how can this civilisation be maintained? What energy powers it? Thirty million people would soon denude the land of timber. And yet there is still global trade: the narrator smokes latakia, a kind of tobacco grown only in a single province of the Ottoman Empire.

Such ideas can seem strong enough to bring down a civilisation but they're secondary, more like a parasite in a body weakened by more deadly bacteria. The fact that they're hatched in disturbed minds makes them even more deadly. In his book, *Intellectuals,* Paul Johnson quoted from poems published in 1841 by the twenty-three year old Marx. "They were entitled *Savage Songs,* and savagery is a characteristic note of his verse, together with intense pessimism about the human condition, hatred, a fascination with corruption and violence, suicide pacts and pacts with the devil." "We are chained, shattered, empty, frightened/Eternally chained to this marble block of being," wrote the poet Marx, and: "We are the apes of a cold God."

In her book *Glittering Images* (2012), Camille Paglia summed up Marxism in this way: "The problem with the Marxist approaches that now permeate academe (via post-structuralism and the Frankfurt school) is that Marxism sees nothing beyond society. Marxism lacks a metaphysics – that is, an investigation of man's relationship to the universe, including nature. Marxism also lacks a psychology: it believes that human beings are motivated only by material needs and desires. Marxism cannot account for the infinite refractions of human consciousness, aspirations, and achievement. Because it does not perceive the spiritual dimension of life, Marxism reflexively reduces art to ideology, as if the art object has no other purpose or meaning beyond the economic or political. Students are now taught to look skeptically at art for its flaws, biases, omissions, and covert power plays."

JJ Rousseau (1712-78) was the great-grand-daddy of all revolutionaries: many of the ideas he set running are still deadly, and becoming yet more deadly with the advancing decay of the West. Environmentalism, for example, came out of his belief in the purity of nature and the vileness of the urban and cultured. He also believed in the perfectibility of mankind, but not in the prissy step by step slowness of the Enlightenment: a single gigantic explosion, the greatest leap forward of them all, was what he had in mind. On top of this, he believed civilisation had corrupted the West by taking people away from a natural and benign sense of self and turning them into selfish creatures full of a self-esteem which they had to bolster by making themselves better than their fellows: richer, wiser, more learned, or just morally superior. Man had therefore been parted from man, each alienated, angry and wanting to do the other down with the result that competition took over from cooperation (Ruskin may have picked up on that one – and he's often called the originator of the Welfare State). Capitalism was the unhealthy outcome. But if people are corrupted by culture then, it follows that, if you alter culture, you can de-corrupt them and undo the damage. And the way to do it is through giving the State unlimited power to compel people to be equal. Anybody who disagrees is wrong, has a false opinion, and should be shut up. "Those who control a people's opinions, control its actions." There'll be no vice, only happiness, when all submit to the State,

Something like a cult grew around his tomb on an island in a lake south of Paris even after his ashes were re-buried in the Panthéon. He's often called the inspiration behind the French Revolution: Robespierre called him 'a teacher of mankind' with a lofty soul. People who knew him personally had other opinions. "A monster who saw himself as the only important thing in the universe" – David Hume. "Vain as Satan, cruel, full of malice" – Diderot. "A pathetic figure and an interesting madman" – Sophie d'Hondetot, the only woman he was said to have ever cared for, on scant evidence. Like all revolutionaries, he had emotional problems of his own – paranoia verging on persecution mania to begin with. The world was out to get him and David Hume was the leader of all the conspirators. 'They' had seen to it that all the coachmen and innkeepers in western Europe were in on the conspiracy, leaving him with no place to hide. He took the manuscript of one of his last books, *Dialogues avec moi-même,* to the high altar in Notre Dame, seeking sanctuary to stop 'them' from destroying it.

The Marquis de Condorcet (1743-1790) had parallel ideas: when reason has perfected us, he said, we'll be practically immortal, speaking a made-up language (designed to make learning easier), living at ease in Elysium. William Godwin (1756-1836) followed: getting rid of private property and marriage will end in global benevolence: benevolence means cheerfulness, cheerfulness means good health, good health means near immortality, cheerfully lived. 'Gracchus' Babeuf (1760-1797) went further in wanting to ban not only private property but high intelligence and skills as well. All would be suppressed to the level of the lowest.

Ideas like these can be very appealing to the right mind. For example, they seem to have affected Percy Bysshe Shelley (Godwin's son-in-law) even though he had mystical experiences of his own and believed that only poetry could make a better world – nothing else would do, not science, reason or religion: he thought, rightly, that poetry should enlarge the mind (or consciousness). "Poetry," he wrote in *A Defence of Poetry* (1821), "lifts the veil from the hidden beauty of the world." In this he was a Platonist, yet in another poem, *Queen Mab,* written when he was twenty-one, the fairy of the title takes Ianthe's soul on a tour of the world's iniquities, all of which are caused by kings, trade and religion. The world they've made is so bad it has to be smashed: destroy the outward and the inward will automatically change for the better. What he didn't know (couldn't know because it hadn't been tried) was that his politics of suppression would make poetry impossible: instead of enhancing consciousness, it would diminish it.

Rousseau's ideas have evolved and changed and nobody really talks about 'Rousseau-ism': not so with Marx. Kenneth Clark, speaking on camera in *Civilisation,* was wrong about

Marxism: failed it had but failure doesn't make a cast of mind change its mind. Marxism morphed, as they say today. In fact it began morphing as soon as intellectuals realised that the proletariat had let them down in the Great War by refusing to obey the laws of Dialectical Materialism: instead of revolting, they'd joined the armies of their own countries. Clark should have spotted the signs. Possibly, even while *Civilisation* was being shot, young revolutionaries had daubed the walls of Paris with three names – Mao, Marx and Marcuse.

Starting in the 1920s, Marcuse, Adorno, Horkheimer, George 'who shall save us from Western civilisation?' Lukacs and others of the Frankfurt School began carrying out the slow-motion revolution which Gramsci had outlined in his concept of the "long march through the institutions" – the infiltration of universities, schools, the church, the judiciary, the media, entertainment (the people now known disparagingly as 'luvvies'). This is Cultural Marxism, designed to bring about the revolution by controlling thought through Critical Theory – endless carping and constant picking on the bad end of every spectrum or, if there is no bad end, making one up anyway.

Not that much of this is all that new. Back in early Georgian England, Bishop Berkeley (not yet a bishop) already understood that language can be a weapon of mass destruction: control language and you control what people think – what they *can* think – and so make them think your thoughts, be obedient to your cast of mind, mindset and outlook. In *Alciphron* (which is, it has to be said, is satirical fiction) the Free-thinkers are already changing the world by re-naming the vices – a crook becomes 'a Man who knows the Ways of the World', a card sharp is a 'Man who plays the Game', 'a vicious Man' (a man, that is, riven by vice) 'is a Man of Pleasure'. The Sect's modern successors have also won the re-naming game, for a time at least.

The Bishop also foresaw the 'long march through the institutions'. Lysicles, the Atheist Free-thinker, says that members of his Sect have been secretly infiltrating society for years – "working like Moles under Ground, concealing our Progress from the Public". Soon the ideas of his Sect, as he calls it, will sprout unaided, untended, in minds which have been already ploughed, planted and weeded. People won't even know what's been done to them as they accept previously alien ideas as their own. But why be secretive? "A Rebellion, or an Invasion, alarms and puts the Public upon its Defence; but a Corruption of Principles works its Ruin more slowly perhaps, but more surely."

Cultural Determinism, based on Darwin, is another idea central to Cultural Marxism – we are animals without souls or hope of an afterlife: what you are is determined by culture, birth, class, race, gender. It's the antithesis of individuality, a regression, a kind of de-evolution back to the pack.

The appeal of single-strand, simplistic ideology can be powerful: it saves you having to think and makes you feel good. Cultural Marxism and Political Correctness are intertwined. As we've seen, the first began in Germany in the 1920s and was taken to the US in the 1930s by refugees from Frankfurt where most of them had worked. PC itself erupted thirty-odd years later, in the 1960s, in American universities. Now it's universal throughout the West but, as I understand it, more especially in the Anglosphere, the ideology of choice of the new élites and their hangers-on: the 1997 New Labour Government in London was the first to be PC through and through – for example, it secretly opened the borders to mass immigration to change the nature of the country, confound Tory voters and buy votes for themselves (since immigrants mostly support Labour).

PC-ness is all about emotion masquerading as reason and it appeals both to the benignly naive and the axe-grinding disaffected, since it poses as caring. Where Marxism was about revolution through economics and the working class, this is wider, taking in whoever it sees as a Victim – women, gays, the disabled, black and brown-skinned people and Muslims. It recognises only one oppressor – pale-skinned middle class males who (apart from their equally pale-skinned accusers) can do no right, while Victims can do no wrong. What began as a demand for tolerance quickly became intolerant of dissent against its own tenets, shutting down other opinions by branding them sexist, racist, Islamophobic and so on. It worked: it works.

In his short book, *The Retreat of Reason* (2006), Anthony Browne pointed out the difference between the politically and the factually correct: the latter can be tested and discarded, rationally, if need be, but P.Correctness is emotional and is always right even when wrong – the truth is what backs up an already held opinion: if the factual truth opposes it, it's branded a lie or dismissed by some other subterfuge, often just blank denial. Statistics come into it a lot.

Browne also suggested it might be something to do with the present age's being a visual one dominated by not very deep celebrities. Reading the written word is almost as solitary as writing it: it's the acme of individualism and just right for laying out arguments: the moving image, in contrast, can be a group thing which is, by its nature, capable of putting over only a very few, very simple ideas, while at the same time being very good at making emotional viewers even more emotional. Like Orwell before him, Browne also suggested this kind of contrarianism might to a rich person's toy and no generation in the whole of history has been as well-off as the Boomers.

The Permissive Society may also have had a separate beginning in Henrik Ibsen (1828-1906) and his plays about doing your thing and letting it all hang out, although the idea of being free to expand consciousness and become fulfilled is much older – like so many things, it dates back to Socrates, Plato and Aristotle. Notwithstanding all that, the Permissive Society as we know it came into being in the 1960s and shouldn't have been faulted – after all growth and the expansion of consciousness is what it's all about: being given permission to expand can only be a good thing. Too often, though, it became a frantic scrabbling back from the terrible void of emptiness at the heart of an unbalanced West. Thoreau put it this way: "The mass of men lead lives of quiet desperation." He added: "What is called resignation is confirmed desperation", but Permissiveness cut out the resignation and tried to blot out the desperation – rock'n'roll too loud for thinking, drugs to blank out the world, and sex the same. As so often it's a question of where you land on the spectrum: the Ancients, for example, also had the idea of the Golden Mean because if you take personal gratification too far you damage other people and that, in turn, diminishes you.

The 1960s also gave us the Greens, starting, most likely, with Rachel Carson's *Silent Spring* (1962), a book about carcinogenic insecticides and weed killer. Some of her claims seem to have been wrong – DDT, it turns out, doesn't thin egg shells although it does kill malarial mosquitoes, but false claims – whether mistaken or wilful – can't stop people of this cast of mind: either they deny they were wrong or, more usually, stay as silent as the coming Spring while working on the next scare. For ten years after *Silent Spring* there was a great hullabaloo over saving the planet and repaying a debt to Nature (or Gaia) which ended with the 1973 oil crisis. Environmentalism took off again in the early 1980s, helped by the release of disappointed but undisillusionable Marxists following the fall of the Berlin Wall and Soviet Russia. In the late 1970s and early '80s, several scares were tried (some with justification) – acid rain, ozone holes, desertification, peak oil, deforestation, population pollution – until they hit on the Greenhouse Effect (later renamed Global Warming and then Climate Change) which was big enough to embrace the entire planet and also had the stamina, and the backing of people making a lot of money out it, to keep on running.

In his book, *Watermelons,* James Delingpole described the Green faith in this way: "The more closely you examine the core tenets of its faith, the more you realise that there is nothing cuddly, fluffy or bunny-hugging about the green religion. In fact, you might not unreasonably describe it as a pagan death cult, rooted in hatred of the human species, hell-bent on destroying almost everything man has achieved, slavishly, weirdly, insanely devoted to a heartless goddess who offers nothing in return, save cold indifference."

It's often said, truly as it happens, that the Nazis were the first Greens with a full-fledged plan for culling what *they* called the wrong or rotten bits of mankind and replacing them with what *they* regarded as good and right ones. The Club of Rome was founded in 1968 by two men – an Italian called Peccei and somebody named Alexander King. During the Second World War King discovered the DDT which his fellow-environmentalist, Rachel Carson, arranged to have banned in the 1960s. By then, King was also sorry for his discovery because it had saved the lives of millions and he'd come to realise that killing them was the way forward. In 1972 the Club of Rome published *The Limits to Growth*, a Malthusian tract proving, through very early computer models, that the the world was out-breeding its ability to feed itself and so it was time to call it a day. 'Humanity is humanity's enemy' and so needs culling, which means by-passing democracy, presumably because, given the choice, not many will choose to be murdered, or even revert to flint knapping and allied Stone Age skills. Environmentalism was the chosen excuse – people have to be culled because people are killing the planet – and in time climate change became the perfect ruse. The only big unanswered question is how do you murder so many, and who buries six and a half billion bodies in a planet-wide charnel house of unburiable and unburnable bones? It'll be Belsen write large, the Killing Fields on a global scale.

On their own they may have been unable to do too much damage, but they had an ally in the United Nations, their head honcho, as it were – Maurice Strong, a self-made Canadian billionaire, a product of a troubled childhood in Alberta, a socialist, and in time Under-Secretary General at the UN. He was he brains behind UNEP and the IPCC but, after the Oil-for-Food scandal in Iraq, turned up in a penthouse in Beijing, making money out the carbon trading scheme he'd helped set up.

More sinisterly, we now have Post-Normal science – the doctrine that it's all right for scientists to corrupt science if by so doing they speed up the fall of the West. This is Lysicles in the lab with his thumb on the scales. Post-Normal Science is new, beginning only in the early 1990s in Leeds University, the idea – or so it seems – of just two masterminds: Jerome Ravetz and Silvio Funtowicz. At least one of the Climategate conspirators was an adherent. It's also sometimes called Noble Cause Corruption which, in accepting it is corrupt, is at least honest

You can read about that corruption in Christopher Booker's *The Real Global Warming Disaster* which, although not about the declining West, can certainly be read that way: not so much declining, in fact, as degenerating into a cat's cradle of deceit and corruption almost as complex as the climate itself, yet characterised by nitpicking pettiness. An Edward Gibbon writing the future *Decline and Fall of the West* might astonish readers (as yet unborn) with a chapter on the banality of the people behind the climate change trick: like the Wizard of Oz, the giants pulling the levers turned out to be lacking in greatness – we're not witnessing the Twilight of the Gods or King Arthur's last weird battle in the West.

People and ideas like these may bring down the West but many are no more than symptoms, not the bacterium. So is there a single cause? We've already listed: over-rationality: loss of a centre: a stalled, stale, stopped society: loss of inwardness: loss of individualism: collectivism: corruption: Corruption of Principles: loathing: self-loathing: disaffection: death through old age: rationalised irrationality: materialism. To which we can add the immaturity of the Boomer generation which has never been quite good enough (and tries to prove its predecessors were never very good, either, by homing in on the worst end of every scale or spectrum they come across). We haven't yet mentioned: structuralism, post-structuralism, modernism, post-modernism, deconstructionism, relativism (nothing is true except the statement 'nothing is true'), multi-culturalism (all cultures are equal except the West's, which is inferior). Missed out also are: sense of moral superiority, resentment, bitterness, envy, snobbery, jealousy, inverted racism, mean-mindedness, unhappy childhoods, refusal to face reality and perhaps even a few phobias. Then there's patriarchy and hierarchy.

There seems, then, to be no single Minotaur at the centre of the labyrinth, only scores of mini-minotaurs in mini-mazes, all interconnected. Or, a better metaphor, we're up against a Hydra with no Heracles in sight. Except at the bottom of all this discontent and mardiness is one simple single cause. What people believe is a factor of a cast of mind, of rationalised emotion, and of a narrowness (or broadness) of understanding or consciousness. And consciousness, I'm arguing, is at the root of it all. People say the West is Judaeo-Christian and up to a point it is but, at its deepest level, it's Greek. Uniquely in the world the Greeks gave us two strands of thought – mind and matter, consciousness and science, the spiritual and the secular, Plato and Aristotle. The two streams are:

Mind/Consciousness/Platonist – Orphism, Pythagoras, Socrates, Plato, Being, Stoics, Plotinus, Erigena, Realists (Duns Scotus), Mystics (Eckhart), Ficino/Renaissance, Bishop Berkeley and immaterialism, Romanticism, German Idealism, Neo-Romanticism, Symbolism, the esoteric.

Matter/science/Aristotelian – pre-Socratics, Becoming, Socrates, Aristotle, Epicureans, Aquinas, nominalists (Occam), empiricism, science, materialism, classicism, the Enlightenment, Marxism/socialism, the exoteric.

The Platonist strand also splits into two: those who claim to have a direct experience of something divine and those (the bulk of any congregation) who believe without knowing. The Aristotelian strand can include mystics as well as atheists but atheists are of course self-excluded from the Platonist wing. To be balanced, you need to belong to both:

the Dark Ages, for example, were unbalanced by the absence of the scientific leg.

Today, however, it's the Aristotelian stream which is too swollen, the Platonist too shrunken and this narrowing of consciousness, I suggest, is the main reason for the decline of the West, the self-destroying hatred at the heart of a single-strand society. It's opened up a pit into which many people fall headlong – Bruegel might have been able to paint it, and them. Others are trying to fill it in with a pseudo-religion promising an earthly paradise, a collectivised utopia. Yet others are just destroyers driven by the rage of Caliban. We may well have passed the point of no return with no hope of re-expanding consciousness, but in the end consciousness is all there is and to thwart it is to destroy yourself.

CHAPTER TWO

Consciousness of Consciousness

Those two Greek streams – the human and the lesser divine – are just two aspects or degrees of consciousness. One theory – that of Bruno Snell (1896-1986) – traced the history of Western consciousness from Homer onwards, though not down to today. According to Snell, it probably all began in a single undifferentiated outward awareness with little inwardness. Or, put another way, back in Homer's day our cultural ancestors had limited self-awareness but a strong sense of being part of the landscape which was in some way sacred, even holy, and which may have imparted a sense of the numinous in a way that only mystics experience today. From there we evolved a sharp and isolating sense of the individual self, an individualised self-awareness.

Our kind of individualist self-consciousness, according to Snell, began to become general in the 7th century BC in Ionia. By the 6th century, spirituality was being internalised and by the end of the 5th century the gods were giving way to human nature as the accepted cause of many of mankind's calamities. The two-stream West began with Plato and the Athenian Enlightenment at the end of the 5th century when he and the people around him had become self-consciousness, though possibly not as fully self-conscious as some people, not all, today.

Snell's *The Discovery of the Mind in Greek Philosophy and Literature* was written as essays for learned journals between 1929 and 1947: three were written and printed during the Second World War. During most of that time Snell was professor of classical philology in Hamburg. Presumably he wasn't a Nazi – the mythology he turned to was Greek not Nordic: Zeus not Woden, Aphrodite not Freya. He also seemed to be pleading for an over-arching Europeanness based on the West's direct descent from a common Greek ancestry. ("We are all Greeks," as Shelley said.)

Homer, said Snell, created both the gods and the Greek literary language. The Olympian gods were conceived, not near Mount Olympus, but in the colonies around the Aegean, at one remove from the bucolic deities of the mainland, such as Gaia and Demeter. The new Olympians were gods of light who got where they did by overturning Cronus (Zeus's father), the Titans and the Giants and in doing so established "the rule of order, justice and beauty". What was overturned was "mere brawn, barbarity, monstrosity and grossness". Nor did the new gods diminish people – they guided and lifted them up to make them less boorish: when men behaved badly, it was because the gods were not there to tell them what to do. The gods made people brave, gave them strength, freedom and self-confidence – Homer's heroes were never abject: the gods didn't demand abasement, although the arrogant always got their comeuppance. Nor was there a flat continuum on Olympus – the gods themselves had their ups and downs because there can be no life in time without change, even life which is immortal.

"European thinking began with the Greeks," said Snell. "They have made it what it is – our only way of thinking." And it began with a Homer who couldn't think exactly like us because he didn't have the words. Greek is remarkable in that many words in use three thousand years ago are still current, though often with changed meanings. (Many obsolete ones survive in English – *hudros* (water) as in *hydrogen,* for example.) *Soma* now means 'body': to Homer it meant 'corpse' – he had no concept of a single living entity because, said Snell, he was aware only of the parts. Figures on archaic Greek vases seem to bear this out: bulbous shins and calves are separated from bulbous thighs by tiny knots of knees. It's the same with arms, torso and head.

Psyche has a similar history: now it means 'soul', then it

31

meant "the force which keeps animals live." It was one of at least eight words for force: *menos,* for example, was that itching feeling or tension you get in arms or legs when you're all pent up and want to to get on with something. Working from words and ideas like these Snell concluded that the Greeks in Homer's time were not all that self-aware: they had no real inwardness but believed they were moved by outside forces, the gods. He quoted the opening of *The Iliad* where Achilles is about to draw his sword on Agamemnon. Instead of deciding for himself that this might be a bad move, Athena had to materialise to stop him: without her, it's implied, he wouldn't have known how to behave.

Nor was happiness inward. The Greeks of the archaic period found happiness in external things – in *olbios* or plenty or profit: more lambs, more olives, a bigger vineyard, victory over the enemy. These things, too, were not in people's own gift – they were given or withheld by an outside force, a Good Demon or *eudaimon.*

But with all of this came an external sense of the spiritual (the mind is lopsided without it): divinity was abroad in the world but not, I think Snell was saying, experienced inwardly, privately. There was little inwardness, little inner life at all. It was the external gods which gave the world meaning because they stood for "serenity, detachment and pure perfection". They were also the deified forces of nature that had to be obeyed: Hera and Aphrodite were spiritualised motherhood and beauty, Artemis and Athena stood for Nature and the intellectual life. They combined "vitality, beauty and lucidity" and the Greeks looked up to them with "wonder and admiration" because they were the perfection of the spiritual life which couldn't be lived on earth: perfection was out there, not in here. (You can also see, I think, the beginning of Plato's Being in all of this.) There was no "sour solemnity" about the gods as there was in the piety of Christianity.

But, Snell contended, as minds evolved they outgrew the gods. "The Olympic gods were laid low by philosophy, but they lived on in the arts", always lessening in divinity until by

Ovid's time in the 1st century AD they were all about "bawdiness and frivolity". These are the gods of the Renaissance, Snell said, an aid against the 'ascetic piety' of the church.

Long before then, however, consciousness had been evolving rapidly. In the one or two hundred years after Homer, Snell argued, the sense of inwardness and individuality had grown immensely, but still only so far. Sappho, a poet of the 7th century BC, knew something of herself but not too much: if things went wrong, she knew she was on her own with no god to help her. She began one poem by saying that the god, Eros, had made her fall in love but a girl who had never had the same godly treatment, and so shunned her. This rejection, said Snell, just made Sappho examine her own inner being without help from the gods.

How strong the evidence for that is, I'm not sure: but there is something else about Sappho which Snell overlooked. There's a radiance about her even in translation (someone – possibly even Plato – called her the Tenth Muse). She speaks of gods – Aphrodite in particular – but she also invests the landscape with a divinity of its own. In one poem she is thinking of her friend and lover, Atthis, who has sailed away to the colony of Lydia on the mainland. Sappho compares her to the moon outshining the stars, throwing its light in whiteness across the salt sea, on to white roses on the island of Lesbos, on to white-flowered chervil and 'honey-clover'. (Sappho was the first, it's said, to call the moon 'silvery'.) This can be read as a poet responding to landscape, imbuing it with a god-free, disbursed divinity, inspired by love. We'll come to Plato later, but this poem can be read as a pre-Platonist Platonic response to the beauty which is in itself spiritual or divine (and which today has largely been lost). Sappho clearly wasn't fully aware of that, of course (Plato, after all, was two hundred years away in the future) but at some semi-conscious level she could have been turning that way.

Pindar, according to Snell's theory, took consciousness to its next stage of evolution – internalising the gods as an inner spiritual experience. He was born late in the 6th century BC, almost exactly a hundred years after Sappho's birth, and lived on into the 5th,, the great age of Athenian civilisation which we also call the first Enlightenment. He was a Theban and Thebes was older than Athens. Thebes, therefore, was rich in myths, gods and heroes. Most of Pindar's works were lost in the Middle Ages and only fragments of his *Hymn to Zeus* survive. On the surface, the poem is about the wives and weddings of Zeus the Saviour, but it was also a record of the birth of the divine forces which keep the world in being. Leto, for example, was the wife who gave birth to Apollo and Artemis. Themis is the goddess-wife who embodies divine order, the right way to do things. Only Cadmus – the founder of Thebes – was mortal, but even mortals have their part to play in the orderly scheme of things: by marrying Harmonia he brought civilisation and discipline to earth.

"What is missing from this beautiful world?" Zeus finally asked the new-born gods. "Divine creatures to praise it," was the reply. So the Muses were born, the daughters of Zeus and Memory. They brought the order and harmony of the arts to earth, to remind people of the beauty of the world and its underlying divinity. The effulgence of that divinity was now in the human mind, I think Snell was saying, and the gods were no longer wholly outside.

But consciousness kept on evolving and being de-spiritualised. By the end of the 5th century, Aristophanes could say that Euripides, spurred on by the thoughts of Socrates, had put an end to tragedy on the stage by killing off the gods. In his play, Medea was a barbarian from Colchis who betrayed her people by helping Jason steal the Golden Fleece. Marriage between them was impossible because Medea wasn't Greek. That left Jason free to marry a Corinthian princess, even though he and Medea by then had two children. In revenge, Medea killed their children and had the royal bride poisoned. No gods were needed: the impetus was pure (impure) human emotion.

"Know Thyself" – written on the lintel of Apollo's Delphic Oracle – seems like an order to look inside yourself yet we're told this is not so: "realise you are a mere brute human, not a god and are far from being one" is apparently what it means. Is that the way Socrates took it? The man who said the unexamined life isn't worth living? His whole system of dialectics was designed to find out what you really know, and to show that you that don't know it anyway. He was aware that common virtues, like justice or courage, were only aspects of a deep single, immaterial *Something* which the mind should be able to reach but never can – it was out of the reach of conscious awareness.

In the *Phaedrus,* Socrates finds himself by the river in the country outside the city walls of Athens. "Dear Pan and all you other gods who dwell in this place," he prayed, "grant me that I may become beautiful within, and that all outwards things I might posses may not war against the spirit within me. May I count him rich who is wise, and as for gold, may I possess so much of it as only a temperate man might bear and carry with him." The inner world was fully there and *oblios* has been discarded. There's not much evidence here, either, that he swayed Euripides towards atheism: he was a theist himself.

It was with Plato, of course, that the Platonic/spiritual stream of Western consciousness really began. What, three hundred years before, had been a spirituality abroad in the world, external to the mind, was now external to the world and internal to the mind which was itself immaterial, belonging to eternity. At the same time, he was well aware of the appetites and their desire, not for the spiritual, but for the earthy and gross: if not watched and kept under, they'd keep you out of heaven. There are, then, two kinds of higher consciousness – an acute awareness of the feeling and thoughts in the mind, and an awareness of a reality outside and beyond it. It only needed Aristotle (following on from the Pre-Socratics) to consolidate the material-type consciousness.

St Augustine (354-430 AD) lived over six hundred years later than Plato and there might be some clues about levels of self-consciousness in his autobiography, *Confessions.* There's the episode with the pear tree, for example. He was sixteen, waiting at home for his father to save enough money to send him to Carthage for further education when one day, out of devilry, he and a gang of boys stripped a pear tree and threw most of the fruit to the pigs. Why? He did evil, he confessed, because of the evil in his mind and because he loved rebellion for its own sake: he didn't want just to be shameless, he wanted to be shame itself, pure and unadulterated. Was he as fully self-aware as we can be (though usually aren't)? As we'll see, Shakespeare could have delved a bit deeper into the saint's psyche and come up with something less generalised than 'evil was the cause'.

A few years before this, Plotinus (204/5–270) most certainly was very inwardly aware. Somebody (somewhere) said that his vision of the cosmos was a copy of what he saw in his own mind. Look inside, he said in the *Enneads,* to see beauty. Like a sculptor, cut away the stone, the bad emotions, to uncover beauty and truth beneath. "Cut away all that is excessive, straighten all that is crooked, bring light to all that is overcast, labour to make all one radiance of beauty". Don't stop "working at the statue until there shines out upon you from it the divine sheen of virtue, until you see perfect 'goodness firmly established in a stainless shrine." Fifteen hundred years later, Hume hadn't advanced even that far – all he saw inside himself was splintered thought, and no self.

In his book, *The World of Late Antiquity,* Peter Brown noted that the art of the late 3rd and early 4th centuries AD was all about the eyes and inwardness. These were eyes through which to see inside the mind of the sitter. What you see is sadness in a dissolving world to which nobody really belonged, an empire of strangers and breaking frontiers. Yet were people like Plato, Plotinus and St Augustine as self-aware as we are? Reading them is like the Turing Test – are you aware of a lower level of conscious in these men? Higher intelligence, of course, and an awareness of the experience of a spiritual dimension which we've now all but lost: but a lower, shallower, less sharp level of self-consciousness? Harold Bloom thought so.

CHAPTER THREE

The Making of the Modern Mind?

Harold Bloom and Owen Barfield were friends who had lunch together whenever Bloom was in London. Barfield (1898-1997) was a pipe-smoking English Public School boy, a solicitor, who'd served in a signals unit of the Royal Engineers in the Great War. He was also one of the founding *Inklings*, that group of writers and academics – including C S Lewis and Tolkien – who met in the Angel and Child in Oxford between the Wars to talk about books, particularly their own (before they were written). Harold Bloom is a loud American academic, a world authority on Shakespeare.

Both thought something had happened to Western consciousness in the 16th and 17th centuries which changed it completely. In Barfield's case, the process took a hundred and fifty years between Copernicus and Newton and it wasn't for the better. For Bloom it all happened in twelve years – between 1594 and 1606 or from *King John* to *Antony and Cleopatra* – because Shakespeare is our creator. They were, of course, talking about those two different aspects of consciousness – Barfield spoke for the lessening of Platonic consciousness, Bloom for an expansion of the Aristotelian kind, a new and deeper understanding of what goes on in our innermost minds. The theory would claim, I imagine, that Plato's consciousness, although closer to ours than to Homer's, was closest of all to the Middle Ages.

Bloom's theory was published in *Shakespeare: the Invention of the Human* in 1999. What he meant by 'human' he never explained. It really just seems to means our present level of consciousness – or, better, our pre-internet level of consciousness. By 'invention' he seemed to mean 'discover,

37

uncover or find out', not something 'made up or put together'. Some time in the latter part of the 16th century the young Shakespeare must have become aware – suddenly or gradually – that people have (or he had himself) a developable inner world, an evolvable inner life, a consciousness which can expand. The mind is not only expandable, not only complex, but also filled with contradictory feelings and thoughts which we can scrutinise and use to understand the motives of both ourselves and of others: the crook and the saint live side by side, in some of us.

Shakespeare was still only in his mid-twenties when he wrote *King John* and created Faulconbridge, the first fictional character in history to show our inner minds to ourselves. That revelation, for Bloom, revolved around these four – rather obscure – lines of Faulconbridge's:

> *But from the inward motion to deliver*
> *Sweet, sweet, sweet poison to the age's tooth:*
> *Which, though I will not practise to deceive,*
> *Yet, to avoid deceit, I mean to learn.*

'Poison', said Bloom, means 'truth'. Faulconbridge has looked inside himself and so knows what goes in the minds of others: he knows why people do what they do. He wants to use this knowledge not to deceive people but to counter their deceit. Later in the play, the French and English Kings agree to a kind of cease fire because both will gain from it. Faulconbridge is outraged, particularly at the Frenchman who dishonoured his country for 'most base and vile-concluded peace'. But why is Faulconbridge so upset? He now knows himself and so also knows why: he'd have gained more personally from war than from peace. Self-awareness had evolved to a wholly new depth.

In similar ways, character after character go on to show people how to look inside their heads to see what's going on in there. Bottom, Mercutio, Portia, Shylock, Richard II all show an 'intensity of being' greater than is needed for a part in a play. Plots aren't needed because these personalities rise above mere action and reveal what's inside them, and therefore inside us also. "They have an interior to journey out from," as we have. As a result they are 'greater than their fates'.

It should be said that Spengler had made a similar point, more briefly, nearly eighty years earlier. Greek plays revolve around a single point of tragedy yet nothing in the inner lives of either Oedipus or Orestes, for example, leads us to that single moment of catastrophic ruin. On the other hand, to understand Othello's downfall you need to know all his past inner life. All the same, Othello's undoing seems more merely personal, parochial almost, less cosmic than the fall of the Greeks – because with them, perhaps, we're dealing with the cosmic aspect of consciousness, not the lower strand of Shakespeare's.

Anthony Burgess had also had a similar insight before Bloom. In his book *Shakespeare* (1970) he located the discovery of the inner mind in *Richard III:* "For the first time, in Clarence's dream speech, the unconscious mind is netted and landed." For both Burgess and Bloom, Hamlet is the highest point reached by humanity. For Bloom, Hamlet was "the most aware and knowing figure ever conceived." He was also: "cold, murderous, solipsistic, nihilistic, manipulative." He was a disunity of opposites – emptiness and fullness – and "veers dizzily between being everything and being nothing". Falstaff is almost equally great. "For Hamlet, the self is an abyss, the chaos of virtual nothingness. For Falstaff the self is everything." To put it another way, each perhaps shows up the extremes of introversion and extraversion. Potentially, Hamlet could have reached Being, lacking only the insight. Falstaff was a Becoming man, locked there forever.

For Burgess people like Falstaff keep civilisation going. Civilisation "disappears when the state is too powerful and when people worry too much about their souls. There is little of Falstaff's substance in the world now, and, as the power of the state expands, what is left will be liquidated." Which offers another explanation for the decline of the West – welfarism, statism, collectivism, leads to the defeat of all the

Falstaffs. Burgess went on: "That Falstaff should be one of the great loveable characters of all literature is – to those who equate lovability with moral excellence – an eternal mystery. But those who see no virtue in war, government propaganda, sour puritanism, hard work, pedantry, Rechabitism, and who cherish fallen humanity when it reveals itself in roguery and wit, then there is no mystery."

Yet Burgess was more limited than Bloom. In Burgess there's no hint of a missing dimension. Bloom, on the other hand, said Shakespeare seemed to be aware of only one of the two streams of consciousness – the human and secular. Could he see the invisible behind the visible? 'Regretfully, no', said Bloom, who'd have preferred a Shakespeare with a vision of the transcendent.

Against that can we put *The Tempest* – if we read it as a kind of allegory of the Platonist vision or view of things. Strip out the cast, except perhaps for a background Prospero, and Caliban becomes a creature of Plato's Becoming, Ariel of Being, the animal versus the divine. The isle's enchanted because of Ariel although he wants to get back to a higher, freer and more aetherial place – but you can hardly have fiction without action and metaphysics is actionless. On the other hand, to back up Bloom, Shakespeare's Sonnets don't reveal the metaphysical side of things, either.

Were Bloom, Spengler and Burgess right? Shakespeare was certainly the first writer that we know of to display the workings of the mind and its emotions. (Though the Wife of Bath is no cardboard cutout.) Four hundred years ago things *did* start to change. Sir Philip Sydney began *Astrophel and Stella* with "... look in thy heart and write". Above all Montaigne invented the essay just to write about himself: "What do I know?" John Florio, who translated Montaigne, knew Shakespeare personally. Did Shakespeare know about Montaigne's essays before they were published, in English, in 1603? People must have talked, if only in the Mermaid Tavern after work. Perhaps Bloom's title should be: *Shakespeare: the Displaying of the Human*.

The new consciousness took time to work through as well: the classicist Enlightenment wasn't all that self-revelatory and the personal had to wait for the Romantics at the end of the 18th century. Even then, poets like Wordsworth still believed in the stiff mechanical psychology of Hartley's Associationism (there was no other). All of this perhaps suggests that other factors were at work and that it would have happened, any way, without Shakespeare. Perhaps the expansion of consciousness had more to do with the Renaissance, the Scientific Revolution, the new habit of questioning and analysing, the invention of the printing press and the take-off the written word, in the vernacular, on a massive scale. Self-knowledge was also given a boost along the way by Rousseau's *Confessions* (1765) which laid bare a human mind at its most prurient and deceitful. (Did he really urinate in that cooking pot? Not straddling the fire, presumably.) In the late 19th century, Ibsen's plays had a similar effect with their themes of personal freedom: he's said, in fact, to have changed not only the Western theatre but the West itself.

You can see all of this happening again with the internet which lets us all look into the minds of millions: many people no longer look at the logic of an argument, only at the psychology of the arguer. Had Marx started out today, for example, his theory would have been read in the light of his personality – his violence, his longing for world-destruction, his sponging (did he ever earn a penny in his life?), his deceit, and the fact that the only working class person he really knew was his maid-servant whom he never paid but did impregnate (he then refused, life long, to acknowledge his son. The boy, I think, was called Fred: a name to scotch any revolution. He *was* working class, though: an engineer-fitter at King's Cross railway station – he died in 1929, twelve years after Lenin put his father's ideas into practice with a bit of mass murder.) Today, the tabloid press would have gone for Marx's boils (he was afflicted from top to bottom, literally), the result perhaps of over-eating, drinking, smoking and physical idleness. A Sage Carbuncular wouldn't have much pull, particularly if the fact that he rarely washed had been thrown in as well. Some might even have noticed his ideas.

And, on top of all that, the matter-strand of consciousness in the West may be changing again – shrinking in this case. In the English-speaking world it may be changing because of the regimenting trend of the last few years. Hayek, following de Tocqueville, warned of the 'democratic despotism' which infantilises people, promising them safety in return for servitude or, to put it most kindly, benign serfdom. Yet things could get even worse. In an article in the London *Daily Telegraph* (6th April 2013), Susan Greenfield, a neuroscientist, suggested that Facebook (to which you could add Twitter) might (possibly, perhaps) change the levels of consciousness of the present twenty-something generation and those below them: inner awareness could contract even more than it has already, replaced by an outward reliance on the opinions of people who are known only electronically. It would be like reverting to the Homeric level of consciousness without the gods: the collective would inflate, the internal atrophy, the external become bloated, the young would grow old living second-hand collectivised impoverished lives. If anything even half like it happens, it really would be the twilight of a West populated by the Eloi of Wells's *The Time Machine*. Who would be the Morlocks?

Snell's wish for the West of the future (our times) would be finally impossible. Without underscoring them, Snell was aware of the two aspects of consciousness and the fact that the West, in this case Nazi Germany, had lost half of its heritage. He advised Germans to follow the "Greek *divinum* rather than Greek *humanum*." He wanted what Pindar had had, a world which was "effulgent with the divine", in which the universal was discernible in the limited, and through which mankind could see the eternal. It had happened in Germany once before. Goethe had turned away from the Age of Reason back to that 'inward glow of Pindar" which is the internalised light of the gods. Goethe turned it into a "secularised faith which traces the divine powers in the workings of nature and

42

in the soul". The city of Thebes, said Snell, had been "spiritually rich and that to a poet is probably far more valuable than the quality we call genius or talent".

Snell was right to worry, just as Bloom and Barfield were both right in the end. Shakespeare, we can concede, was the first modern man – fully self-aware but with no personal experience of the spiritual dimension. All the same, materialism – the belief that nothing exists but matter – has gained a lot of ground since then. With it has come its own dilemmas – how, for example, does it explain the immateriality of thought?

CHAPTER FOUR

The Concrete Cul-de-Sac

In 1974 the American philosopher, Thomas Nagel, asked himself "what is consciousness?" and his mind turned to bats – the ones which navigate the night by asdic. "Is there something it is like to be a bat?" You can describe in detail a bat's taxonomy, count the genes in its DNA, rake through its stomach to see what it's eaten but you can never know what it's like to be a bat, get inside its head to see and hear as a bat does. This fairly obvious observation, apparently, was enough to get people interested in researching consciousness, something which 20th century psychology had largely ignored: from 1913 until the 1970s, Behaviourism by-passed it altogether, focusing instead on how people act, how Pavlov's dogs behave, what rats do in mazes. Rival psychologies, such as Gestalt, were more like therapies looking at the whole mind, not the parts.

In 1994, the Australian philosopher David Chalmers reckoned the problems facing psychology could be split into two: a solitary hard problem (how can matter make non-matter?) and a lot of easy ones (how does memory work? how do we pay attention?). Patricia Churchland said it's a 'hornswoggle problem' (*to hornswoggle,* 1829, to cheat) because, given time, the mind-matter problem might be easily solved while the apparently easy ones which may never be. Others thought the problem was neither hard nor soft, just insoluble: people who think this way are called *mysterians.*

What is consciousness made of? Roger Penrose and Stuart Hammeroff, an anaesthesiologist, offered a quantum solution: inside each brain cell is a microtubule connecting the macro-world to a quantum one, perhaps like worm holes in space-time. And consciousness? No answer to that. Susan Greenfield thought it all a matter of scale – any critical mass of neurons in a network will create consciousness automatically. How? No answer, either. Mystifyingly, Stephen Pinker thought: "Computation has finally demystified mentalistic terms". Daniel Dennett thought consciousness is going on non-stop in parallel streams – it's just that we can pay attention to only one at a time. What is consciousness? "A bunch of tricks."

Some say there's no flowing self, only bundles (bunches?) of splinters. There are ego theorists (the self exists) and bundle theorists (it doesn't). Most religions are based on ego theories, only Buddhism is the bundle kind. Susan Blackmore thinks both self *and* consciousness are illusions – an illusion being something which exists but isn't what it seems: Necker cubes are illusions.

As for *why* consciousness evolved, there seem to be three schools of thought: it's a useful adaptation to the world: it's a useless by-product of a useful adaptation to the world: it's something else. But is it needed? Could we get along without it? In 1994, Todd Moody asked: what if each of us has a clone, almost a replica except our zombie-copies lack consciousness? Could a third person tell the two of us apart? Can you have complex thoughts and ideas and not be aware of them? More to the point (and I'm not sure if this question was asked) could they create a complex society? Could computers?

The zombie question isn't new. Bishop Berkeley had a version of it in the early 18th century, in the long peace of the Augustans. How do you know that the people all around you have consciousness? If you think they have, that makes God's existence – the Greatest Consciousness – all the more likely, a conclusion unwelcome today, I imagine.

In 1982 the Australian philosopher, Frank Jackson tried to counter the materialist – or physicalist – view of the universe with a thought experiment. Mary is a futuristic neurophysiologist who knows all that can be known about

45

colour and vision. She's been brought up from birth in a black and white locked room. (I suppose we have to assume she isn't colour blind and has never combed her hair in a mirror, never seen her own red mouth, or her brown, grey or blue eyes). Then she's let loose into a coloured world. Although she'll know the words for sea-green, sky-blue and moon-yellow, will something new and immaterial be added to her consciousness when she sees colour for the first time? Is there, in other words, more to the world than mere matter?

Chalmers said yes, the case against pure materialism had been made. Dennett said his reasoning was flawed. If Mary knew everything, then she'd already know the effect on her rods, cones, retina and brain of energy at that wavelength. (Erwin Schrödinger – who'd died twenty years earlier – thought physics never would understand the 'sensation of colour'.)

Another thought experiment tests whether or not you believe in a separate self. Imagine Scottie in *Star Trek* beaming up Kirk from an alien planet. After being scanned – and the code in his DNA extracted – Kirk's atoms are discarded. The onboard computer takes a new set of atoms and uses the (immaterial) DNA code to turn them into Kirk. Is the new Kirk the same as the old? Has his 'self' survived obliteration and a kind of replication? Would *you* step inside the transporter chamber and let yourself be disassembled and reassembled out of different atoms? Would you be afraid that the real you would die?

The unasked question in all of this, of course is: "can you have a science of consciousness?" It doesn't lend itself to experiment – there's not a lot to measure or put in a test tube. Too many scientists seem to have limited levels of whatever consciousness is: the Platonic dimension is, seemingly, closed to them. Not unnaturally, therefore, a lot of research is about how the brain works: blindsight, the cutaneous rabbit, agnosia, synaethesia, inattentional blindness, change blindness. A lot, it seems, has to do with sight: an example dates from the Second World War when barrage balloons floated over London tethered by steel cables. People could 'see' the cables even when in fact they couldn't because too few photons reached the eye. The brain filled in the gap.

On the whole. we've gained very little from this research – except for two useful new words: *quale* and *qualia* (the plural) are from the Latin for 'what kind" and their English meanings were coined, I think, by the American philosopher, Ned Block. They mean what you and you alone are conscious of – a headache, for example, what a symphony does to you, or how you see colours. (How often do different people give different names to the same colour – is this purple or mauve, pink or pale red?) *Qualia* are the great unknowables because each man really is an island: Shakespeare's discovery of the modern mind can never go deep enough to end all isolation. What's missing today is any widespread awareness that *qualia* can include spirituality. Modern consciousness has, in this way, shrunk and the recent search for proof that thought is a by-product of matter is a factor of its loss. Materialism is nothing new, pre-dating as it does any concept in the West of immateriality – and yet the materialist philosophies of Antiquity all had their divine sides: this shrinkage of consciousness is entirely modern.

CHAPTER FIVE

Materialism and the Light of Eternity

People say that Epicurus (341-270 BC) was a thorough-going materialist and he probably thought so himself. There was, however, more to him than that. From Democritus – who died thirty years before he was born – he took the idea that all that ultimately exists are atoms perpetually falling through a void. Now and then, like a Butterfly Effect, some veer slightly from their straight downward fall to gather together into random and short-lived solids – the cosmos and all that's in it. After a while, the atoms break apart and the thing that was is no more. The fall of atoms goes on forever.

Some of that is thoroughly modern and could – with a little tweaking to take in quantum physics – almost sum up the beliefs of millions in the West today. Except Epicurus also believed in gods who lived in the interstices between the atoms and so were incorruptible because only what is made from matter can be corrupted. Also, because they live between the falling atoms, the gods are immortal, but not supernatural: they're Being Itself, abstract existence, in its purest possible form – they have to exist in order to actualise that abstract perfection of being which reason tells us must be real. Perception of the gods is wired in, so they have to exist – an earlier ontological argument than St Anselm's, and just as wrong. They're self-sufficient, self-absorbed in the bliss of pure being, unaware of matter and so they can't interfere with us because they don't know we're around. And they're completely immaterial, neither creators nor created, just the highest point that being itself can possibly reach. They're beautiful in the same way that some people are, but they aren't projections – they exist outside us. Wise people contemplate them as the highest good, praise them in prayer, expecting nothing in return.

So Epicurus believed that although we vanish completely on death, while we're here we can touch eternity, and see – in a single take of the eye – all that has been, is, and will be. More than that, this sense of touching the essence of being can be cultivated, and should be. He not only believed in immateriality – the abstract purity of being – he encouraged his followers to reach up to savour the beauty, peace and immortality of the gods through spiritual exercises and the serenity which comes from controlled thought – the standard trick for inducing mystical experiences worldwide. For this reason, his followers were taught to memorise and internalise the Epicurean dogmas, particularly the Fourfold Remedy ("they will be your companions and free you of worry"): the gods aren't fearful/death isn't dreadful/the good is easy to get/the bad is easy to bear. Contemplate these ideas. Horace, the Epicurean Roman poet of the 1st century BC, added: go for a walk in the woods and turn these words over in your mind. Think about death and value life.

Controlling thought, I think Epicurus realised, really means emptying the mind to let it be filled by an awareness of the infinity of the cosmos, the greatness of the gods. Lucretius, the Epicurean Roman 1st century BC poet, has a passage where the walls of the world are split and the poet sees all the things of the void hurtling about. "I find myself seized by a kind of shudder of divine pleasure." Like all the philosophies of Antiquity, Epicureanism was a way of life, lived in a school, with the intention of changing people inwardly. A quiet mind is needed and each school – there were several around the Roman Empire – ran confessionals to rid people of guilt, a prime source of pain and unhappiness. Look at the world in the light of its immensity and cultivate detachment, change what you think is important.

Epicurus was born perhaps only six years after Plato died yet Plato belonged to the 5th century Enlightenment, while Epicurus was Hellenistic, the time when Alexander spread the Greek language and Greek thought from Egypt to Afghanistan, destroying the old city states as he did so. With them, some people think, went an homogeneous Greek civilisation and with it a sense of belonging. The world was now bigger and more hostile: Stoicism had roughly the same starting date and it was also the age of the Cynics and Sceptics, people coping with change and helplessness.

Epicurus was from the Athenian colony on Samos – an island famous as the birthplace of Pythagoras, Aesop, Aristarchus (the first to notice the earth goes around the sun) as well as Epicurus. (In the 6th century Eupalinos dug a tunnel – an aqueduct, in fact – half a mile long through a mountain.) Being an Athenian, Epicurus did his military service in that city's army. Then, after the death of Alexander the Great, the citizens of Samos were exiled to Colophon in what is now Turkey. Epicurus taught for a time in Mytilene, Sappho's old home town, then founded a school in Lampsacus in the Dardanelles before going back to Athens to set up his final school in a house and garden between the Academy and the Stoa. His is a philosophy best fitted for a garden, and friendship – friendship above all: each school was a home for the like-minded (free men, women, and slaves) at ease in a garden.

Nowadays Epicurus is characterised – on the rare occasions he's thought about at all – as a hedonist. He was no hedonist. More mildly, it's said he favoured pleasure as the highest good. What Epicurus was really about, I think, was getting rid of mental pain to let peace settle in, a mind at peace with itself. People spoil things for themselves by wanting more than they can have, being dissatisfied with what they have, fearing to lose what they have. Once you've achieved peace (or pleasure), freedom from abject want is all you'll need: you can't add to peace or make it bigger, it's complete in itself. Meanwhile, be happy by avoiding what causes pain and upset – public life, soldiering, wrangling, other people. So, like your atoms, adhere to like-minded people in a garden and take everything slowly and in moderation – over-eating causes pain, for example, so don't do it.

Fear of death drives the appetites and upsets a tranquil state of mind, but death is a complete ending – that random gathering of millions of tiny inert atoms, which are you, disperse never to be seen again or repeated. Epitaphs on tombstones around the Roman Empire were often inscribed with an epigram translated into Latin from the Epicurean Greek: "Non fui, fui, non sum, non curo". 'I wasn't, I was, I'm not, I don't care.'

Nobody is totally original and many of the ideas of Epicurus clearly come, not only from Democritus, but from Socrates too: don't do wrong and don't retaliate for wrongs done to you, for example. He's said to have influenced modern science. By its nature, Epicureanism was never meant for the masses, more for small coteries, and it didn't survive, not intact anyway, very far into Late Antiquity which is usually dated from 200 to 700 AD. But it wasn't forgotten. A Greek doctor, Asclepiades, took Epicurean medicine to Rome in the 2nd century BC. It was based on keeping the body in balance since illness is caused by irregularities in the flow of atoms (as well as the blockage of pores). The cure was a balanced diet, massage, exercise, clean clothes and clean bodies.

Horace (son of a freed slave) was often translated or imitated in late 17th and early 18th century England. Because of this, Epicureanism had some effect on the Enlightenment in Queen Anne's time. Pope's *An Essay on Criticism* is practically Horace's *Ars Poetica* in English heroic couplets. The Enlightenment concept of Horatian grace and being at ease among educated friends was something learned from the Greek philosopher via the Roman poet. Some say Epicurus helped to shape Locke and so also the Founding US Fathers, as well as Hume. Marx, a congenital materialist, wrote his PhD thesis about Democritus and Epicurus. Epicurus also made an impression on both Schopenhauer and Nietzsche, without noticeably cheering them up. Dante stuck him, a bit unfairly, in the Inferno (Level Six) for his materialism.

On his death-bed he passed his own test: he was a fortnight dying, in great agony but cheerfully, of dysentry and a kidney stone which stopped him urinating. At the same time he arranged for the care of the children of a friend.

Epicurus showed up the contradictions in materialism: all is matter except for those abstractions – like existence itself – surrounding it. More than that, those immaterial ideas could change matter. And Epicurus wasn't the only one. Matter was also Aristotle's stock in trade. We think of him as a kind of research scientist, logician and zoologist and the man who had original ideas about metaphysics, physics, ethics, politics and the arts. Yet Plutarch said he lifted philosophy off the earth into the realm of *epoptics* – revelation of the transcendent as in the Eleusinian or Orphic Mysteries. He was, in fact, a man to whom the most important things were immaterial.

In the Gifford Lectures of 1914, Dean Inge noted that materialism is reductive, always boring down to find the smallest bits of matter, while Aristotle looked at the developed whole. Materialism, said the Dean, looks at existence without putting a value on it, ignoring the 'perceiving mind' altogether: Aristotle, on the other hand, thought that the eternal Mind and also what is best in people are one and the same thing: the intellect is both essential to mankind on earth and yet at the same time is divine. What is most truly human rises above the human. Study, learning, knowledge raises you to this universal state.

If the Pythagorean way to the divine was through mathematics, Aristotle's was through learning – and not just about a single subject: you need a well-stocked mind and for that you need to know what Matthew Arnold later called 'the best of what's been thought and said'. Aristotle's way called for mental or intellectual activity – everything else is secondary – but at the same time, you're on your own, self-dependent, though you need leisure, freedom, detachment, and few worries. The model is God, defined as 'thought which thinks with no interest in anything outside itself' and which we can think of as pure consciousness. Research and study can by themselves invoke mystical experiences. Getting the answer right isn't always necessary, either: probability can be enough. (The unasked question is: will any kind of knowledge work? Astrology as well as astronomy?)

He also knew there are different levels of experience: happiness comes through the research itself while beatitude comes only occasionally and on contact with the divine. "Like is known only by like", he said: in other words, we can know the divine, because something in us is also divine. Not only that but the divine is everywhere, numinous and universal. Aristotle told the story of visitors who found Heraclitus warming his hands at the fire in his kitchen and not in the living room (which was dedicated to Hestia, the goddess of the heath) where he'd normally meet guests. "Come in, there are gods in here too," said Heraclitus, because all creation is sacred. (Why do we shy away from the ugly bits of nature, Aristotle asked, and yet we don't when we see them in paintings? (Art was becoming more demotic at the start of the Hellenistic age.))

In the end, Aristotle believed, the only true knowledge is immaterial and unchanging, as in the Forms (but not the Forms of Plato). At the bottom of all material things is something he called – or we do in translation – *Substance*. *Hypo-stasis* was the word Aristotle used. As we'll see later, the early Church Fathers applied it to the Trinity and Tertullian translated it literally into Latin as *sub-stantia*, hence our 'substance' – a bad word to use in this context since its regular English meaning confuses what Aristotle was trying to say. The Greek literally meant 'under-standing', 'under-pinning', 'under-neath', 'under-lying' in the sense, perhaps, of free-standing, needing nothing else for its own existence or support. Put like that, Aristotle's Substance both makes more sense and at the same time loses it – all it says, in effect, is 'there's something unknowable out of which all things are made'. By it Aristotle meant undetectable matter out of which all detectable things are made by the Forms.

53

A rough analogy could perhaps be with clay. Suppose clay is the *hypostasis* which we can't see or touch until an abstract immaterial idea turns it into a brick, a pot, a statue, gives it a shape and make it touchable. More realistically, perhaps *hypostasis* is like the energy which is shaped by abstract immaterial rules (the Forms) into the things of the universe – still not an exact comparison because we can measure energy. The soul, an image of God, shapes the body though it can't be extracted except in thought. When the body ends, it ends. But where did these short lived Forms come from if they weren't eternal? What made them? Whatever the answer, Aristotle believed that, although matter is our primary concern, there is something else, and that something is immaterial.

The end also drives the beginning. What comes first – the chicken or the egg? The potential of the chicken comes first, I suppose, or the immaterial idea of a hen. The idea of the oak creates the acorn to actualise the potential held in the idea of oak.

Forms actualise what is potential – and in that concept we have the clue to the purpose of Aristotelian life, which is eudemony or a life well lived. It means becoming what we were meant by nature to be: the good life is lived when what was immaterial potential in us has been actualised. We can be happy only when all our capacities, capabilities and talents are fulfilled and we become virtuous, where virtue means fineness or excellence of character. The end result, the highest point, is wisdom. You should then be contented, fulfilled, flourishing, serene and therefore of use to your society – a carrier, not the carried. You should also train yourself to live by the Golden Mean – not rashness, for example, nor cowardice but somewhere in between.

Politically, it therefore follows that the State's job is to enable eudemony to happen by getting out of the way. A government's authority ends when it will (or can) no longer do so. Social engineering is therefore wrong and anti-Aristotelian. Trying to change human nature to fit a template which suits your cast of mind is not only impossible but wicked because it stops other people from evolving.

Aristotle's belief that science can grow the soul was shared by Cicero (106-43 BC), the man who civilised the Latin language (his writing style was copied down to the 19th century), who brought Greek philosophy to the Romans thereby saving a lot of the lesser kind for us, the originals of which have been lost. Caesar applauded him for widening the Roman mind, a better thing than widening the Empire's bounds. In a letter, Seneca the Younger (1-65 AD) wrote that you can find divinity – Wordsworth's 'intimations of immortality' – in dense forests of tall and ancient trees. If you find a deep cave, divinity will invade your soul. We venerate the source of great rivers. Hot springs have altars. The sacred, in other words, is numinous. You'll also find the divine in the man who is serene whatever happens to him.

Both Cicero and the two Senecas (Older and Younger) were Stoics, followers of the fourth great Greek philosophy of Antiquity and a materialist one as well. Its founder, Zeno (334-262), born in Citium (present day Larnaca in Cyprus) was only seven or eight years younger than Epicurus. So close together were they in time, and so important was Athens, that the school and garden of Epicurus lay between Plato's Academy and Zeno's Stoa. (Stoa meant a 'colonnade' – Zeno taught in one called the *Stoa Poecile,* the painted porch.)

If today's materialist/atheist élite ever feel the need for a religion, they might find it ready made in Stoicism. High class Romans followed it because of its moral teaching, its code of rationality, moderation, tolerance. Most of the things which happened to us are beyond our control, except the one and only thing which matters – our attitude to death and calamity: nothing can hurt you unless you let it, hence our word 'stoical'. 'Materialism, monism, mutation' is sometimes said to sum up Stoicism because of its belief that the universe is made of a single stuff which constantly changes. That single, simple matter is Heraclitean fire envisaged as something very fine like attenuated flame or heat, or our energy. Stoics called it Logos, Reason, Mind, Nature, Fate, Providence, Law, Necessity, Zeus or God. It is, therefore, rational even though it explodes out of nothing in a gigantic red hot Big Bang. It cools into earth, air, fire and water which in turn shape all the things of the world, including people who also keep a bit of the rationality of this exploding Logos inside them: we are therefore part of the universe and share its intelligence, somewhat diluted. (The Universal Intelligence is impersonal and has nothing to do with us.)

The earlier Stoics thought that after a while (a very long while) the explosion/expansion will slow, stop, and rush back into a Big Crunch or Conflagration, before exploding once again to re-create every last bit and particle of the same old universe. This it does forever and ever. Presumably this is where Nietzsche got the idea of 'the eternal recurrence' from.

For the Stoic, the aim of life was happiness through living according to the laws governing the nature of things. You have to evolve into what Nature intended you to be. Suicide was fine and in fact Zeno killed himself. It's all very pantheistic but it means that, because you and everything else are made of the same stuff, you should be kind, tolerant, forgiving and helpful to everybody else. The Cynics, I think, coined the word 'cosmopolitan' to describe the typical Stoic – a citizen of Cosmos City, an idea better suited to an empire of strangers than a city state of similar people. Stoicism was open to all, male or female, slave or free. Epictetus (55-135 AD) had been a slave: Marcus Aurelius (121-180 AD) was the Emperor who learned from him.

Like all the great Greek philosophies Stoicism was far from being an academic subject: it was a way or life, not only with words and ideas to live by, but also with its own spiritual exercises to induce moments of mystical contact with the divine. It couldn't last, however, and ended in sadness brought on by the emptiness and futility of it all. (It's said that the ethos of 19th century English Public Schools was modelled on Stoicism.) Barbarism was too much in the end,

I suppose. Marcus Aurelius spent more time fighting barbarians in the great reed marsh in the Danube estuary than is good for any emperor: the horizon, only a foot away, isn't horizontal but vertical, a rustling swaying wall of green and grey reeds higher than the tallest man's head. The emperor said: "You are only a little soul carrying a corpse about." In a way it foreshadowed the decay of the West because, in the end, there was nothing positive to believe in, nothing quite alive about it. In that, also, it was like Aristotle's Unmoved Mover which, although it can be thought of as thought and life itself, also seems to have been invented because logic dictated it: although Dante made something splendid out of it – the Love which moves the stars and lesser planets but, then, art's business is to expand consciousness, one way or another.

CHAPTER SIX

The Uses of the Arts

The sole point of art is to expand consciousness. It has no other purpose. Good art expands it: bad art shrinks people inwardly. Today in the West too much art is bad, too narrowly political, too intent on criticising society or harping on the dark end of the human spectrum. It's a sign of distress, if not of outright decline: a society whose art is bad can't by definition be good – it's bad because it's abandoned its proper function of expanding consciousness. This has become a querulous, petty and petulant society with too many discontented people intent on destroying it (discontented because of a contracted consciousness).

Art expands consciousness in three ways, which, of course, match our two strands of consciousness: the lower two are all about the here, now and human psychology: the higher connects directly to the higher itself. At the lowest level, novels can take you to places otherwise closed to you. They can be plotless and one-dimensional yet still expand consciousness: C S Forester's Hornblower stories, for example, leave you almost with *memories* of life in frigates and ships of the line in the Nelsonic sailing navy.

The second level is also mainly literary, doing to the individual what Bloom said Shakespeare did for us all – expand consciousness by letting you see inside other minds, either strangely alien or just like ourselves laid bare. In knowing them, your own mind is expanded.

The highest kind of art is on different level altogether, no longer about the human but the divine – in other words the realm of Being because through it you can sense the 'invisible beyond the visible'. At this level, literature usually gives way to painting or – more especially – music. Poetry can work, though verse which is good enough is rare. "Finish, good lady, the bright day is done and we are for the dark".

Art at the third level, in fact, is not only rare but nowadays rarely understood. So rare is it, in fact, that we have to go back to the Victorians to find out what it's all about – in, for example, the artistic evolution of Gauguin. In the 1870s, he was an Impressionist: Impressionists, he said, painted what the eye could see but not the mystery inside the thing painted. In the 1880s, he became a Symbolist or what he called a Synthetist. Mallarmé summed up Symbolist painting: "peindre non la chose, l'effet qu'elle produit." 'Don't paint the thing, paint the effect it has on you.' In the 1890s, Gauguin was in Tahiti painting what to Europeans was still a very far away place, vivid with tropical colour. By now he was saying: "The essence is what is not expressed". Or, in other words, the point of a painting is to reveal the divine.

There is one way, and one way only, to reach this highest level – and that is through beauty, and the invariable and inevitable mood of 'sadness and repose' it brings with it. (This was Ruskin's insight.) Centuries ago, Japanese *haijins* isolated four essential moods – sadness for the loneliness, brevity, strangeness or greaterness of things. Latin has *lachrymae rerum*, tears for things, English has nothing. But beauty – something beautiful – comes before the sadness. For this reasons I think Gauguin was wrong about the Impressionists. What they painted was a kind of beauty and, as we've seen, that is all you need.

Why should beauty work like this? Plotinus had no doubts: beauty alone gets you to Being because Beauty *is* Being, therefore earthly beauty must take you back to where it comes from – both are one and the same thing. Not all souls see this, he added, but those which do 'reascend' to the source of us all. "Chiefly," Plotinus wrote in the *Enneads,* "beauty is visual. Yet in word patterns and in music (for cadences and rhythms are beautiful) it addresses itself to the hearing as well. Dedicated living, achievement, character, intellectual pursuits are beautiful to those who rise above the realm of the senses: to such ones the virtues, too, are beautiful." Beauty you also find in the well-stocked mind, in bravery, in ideas, and in skills (manual or otherwise). Love itself is a response to beauty.

Pure single colours are beautiful and can have a spiritual effect, Plotinus went on to say. Some of Rothko's floating panels of colour bear this out. *Black on Maroon* (1958) works, I think. Although it's set in a maroon background, from a distance it seems to be a black rectangle surrounding two narrow strips of maroon separated by a black bar like the mullion of a window. It's as though you're looking through a black-walled prison cell and then through a window into a maroon infinity. (Not like that 'little tent of blue', but a maroon eternity.) Closer up, the frame and mullion are blurred and shaky in a not quite earthly way. This fuzziness could help. Mondrian also dealt in squares and oblongs of pure colour but with straight edges and black dividing lines. He doesn't work as well as Rothko and perhaps that straightness is the reason why – it's all too regimented.

On the whole Plato, often seemed a bit unsound on the fine arts but Athens in the 5th century BC was city of paintings, plays, sculpture, statues, architecture, and poetry. When no plays were being staged, dealers set up stalls in the theatre, selling books for a drachma a copy at a time when the sea passage from Egypt cost two. A drachma was worth around £80 in today's money. Books were therefore dear but there was a market for them.

Socrates's father was a sculptor/stonemason (we'd call him an artist, his contemporaries called him a workman) and Pheidias's great ivory statue of Athena in the Parthenon was carved in his son's lifetime. A statue of a boy charioteer was cast in bronze in the 470s around the time Socrates was born. It was made for Apollo's shrine at Delphi and was buried there by an earthquake until unearthed in 1896. The boy's eyes seem to see eternity: his body, in a long pleated gown, is preternaturally still, not so much stiff as embodying stillness.

The face, too, is sad and so we have here the Ruskinian formula of sadness and repose cast in bronze two and half thousand years ago.

Plato's objection to some of the arts was probably political – their effects can be anti-social. For himself, he seems to have thought highly of poetry. Ion, in the dialogue of that name, was a rhapsode, a professional reciter of other people's poetry. He was from Ephesus but travelled all over the Greek-speaking world reciting poetry, mainly Homer's (all of which he'd memorised), at festivals and in private houses for fees and prizes. Poets, said Plato, don't write poetry – a god speaks through them: the poet is a conduit, an amanuensis taking the verses down by dictation.

In 1985, Benjamin Libet proved that muscles begin to move before the mind has framed the command. Would this have surprised Plato? Poets are often surprised by what they've done – words and ideas just seem to appear out of nowhere. No true poetry is composed consciously, just written down (and worked over later). The unconscious, including inspiration, is by its nature hidden but without taking it into account how can any science of consciousness be complete?

Ion, too, Plato said, was taken over by the gods when he was in full flow in his robes and golden crown standing raised above the crowd reciting Homer in a competition in a festival. Poets are like rings of iron, Socrates told him, which the gods have magnetised: each ring attracts and magnetises other iron rings – the rhapsodes – and, through them, the audience who hear them recite. Each person is a link in a chain of inspiration connecting them to the gods. Art is therefore divine.

The Greeks didn't have a word for 'art' in our sense. Instead they used *techne,* which is more like professional knowledge: inspiration is something higher. People who work well in any area can be inspired. When possessed, Socrates tells us in the *Ion*, the Bacchics ladled up milk and honey from rivers of water. In the same way "poets gather songs at honey-flowing springs, from glades and gardens of the Muses. They bear songs to us as bees carry honey. A poet is an airy thing, winged and holy, and he not able to make poetry until he becomes inspired and goes out of his mind and his intellect is no longer in him. Therefore it's not by mastery that they make poems but by a divine gift."

Apart from this, neither Plato nor Plotinus had a theory of art. They didn't need one – beauty in any shape is all that's needed to get you to Being or, in the case of Plotinus, Mind. The concept of Fine Art, and so also aesthetics, came with the 18th century and the Age of Reason. According to Paul Oskar Kristeller, it was through Kant that the old Platonic Forms of Beauty, the Good and the Truth ended up as aesthetics, ethics, epistemology. Whitehead's professors had arrived and the Platonist strand of consciousness had become something to analyse and study, divorced from any sense of the divine.

Aristotle's opinion of tragic poetry is well known and so is now a bit tedious: he thought it cathartic, purging playgoers by exposing them to the worst and most terrifying emotions from a place of safety on the stone benches of the theatre. Art expands consciousness by shock, perhaps. It works: Lear or Oedipus stay in the mind, lessons in not defying the nature of things. Poetry, said Aristotle, is more important than factual history because it's about what could happen, not what merely has. Art is about the universal.

5th century BC Athens was also rich in playwrights, three of whom are still staged from time to time two and half thousand years later, and this was the society which made the West. But, as Ruskin pointed out, only great societies have great art because art reflects great societies, in a mildly positive feedback loop. Walt Whitman also said that great poets need a great audience. Without it – without them – there can be no great art. I suspect, as well, that because of these factors, greatness comes in spikes.

Roger Scruton has said something similar: high culture and high art are essential for society's survival. They're needed for emotional maturity. Today, both have failed, replaced by the ersatz – ersatz emotions, fake art. For the false to win, the enemy has to get rid of any concept of objective truth – the argument between Socrates and the Sophists is still being played out, with the sophists easily winning at the moment. Today they're helped by Marxism and Foucault-ism (truth is what the rulers say it is in order to keep the ruled in order).

Spengler, writing in 1918, must have had something similar in mind when he forecast the demise of the West – he said the newly established avant-garde was turning against its own society and tearing it apart. Except this wasn't true of English Modernist writing – not intentionally, at least: Eliot, after all, was a pin-stripe and spats man, a banker and a publisher. Ezra Pound inveighed against the West – "an old bitch gone in the teeth ... a botched civilisation" – but he also quoted Mallarmé in translation: we need to 'purify the dialect of the tribe' in order to revive poetry until 'change hath broken down/All things save beauty alone". Imagism, in Pound's mind, was an attempt to break free of space and time and vault to a higher level of consciousness, propelled by the power of an image, unhindered by too many words. (Imagist poetry was based on a misunderstanding of haiku, about which not a lot was known in the early 20th century but which, because it's spiritual in nature, could barely be understood in the modern West.)

The rage against the West in art began before World War One. Expressionism began in Germany in 1905: what it expressed was the disturbed mind. Munch's *The Scream* is best known and sums it up. At it's best, however, it's still an insight into other minds – or your own – and so able to amplify consciousness. Dadaism, which began in the Great War in Switzerland (a neutral country) is the obvious example of what Spengler had in mind. Duchamp pencilled a moustache on a copy of the *Mona Lisa* and hung a urinal on a wall as a work of art. Today's infantilism seems to have begun in that act of childishness – though, it has to be said, if anybody's consciousness is stretched by looking at this kind of stuff, I suppose, it must qualify as art if only for them and nobody else.

Some Dadaists joined the Surrealists in the 1920s. Surrealism means beyond reality, extra reality, extreme reality, above reality – though it was too attached to those two materialists, Freud and Marx. It was in fact a collective of group-thinking free-thinkers. Overturning the middle classes through art was their intent. At the time, they didn't overthrow anything but they did make some very fine and Platonically sound art along the way. Take, for example, Magritte's 1933 oil painting, *The Human Condition*. It's a perfect example of why Plato was wrong about art being a copy of a copy of something in Being and therefore of no mystical use. It's a painting of a painting on an easel in front of a window. The painting is a perfect copy of the scene outside – a tree and bushes in the foreground, a wood, possibly on a hill, stretching away in the background, under a summer blue sky with well-painted clouds. But the painting on the easel covers only about a third of the window and if it weren't for the edge of the canvas you'd never know it was there – the painting of the scene and the scene itself are perfectly matched. So exactly so that you feel if you took away the canvas you'd leave a hole in the landscape. It proves a copy of a copy can get you at least half-way to Being.

Some date Modernism from 1913 and the Armory Show in New York which outraged President Roosevelt: "That's not art." On show were examples of Fauvism, Futurism and Cubism. Outrage has been common ever since. But I think it was Larkin who said there must be something wrong with avant-garde music because it has never caught on even decades after it was written. Some things really are outrageous and *la bourgeoise,* as well as being easily *épaté,* can sometimes get it right.

Plato, who had doubts about letting poetry loose in the ideal cities of Kallipolis and Magnesia, thought the right kind of music could be a good thing. Centuries later, Plotinus recognised that even a single note can lead the listener back to Mind. But neither Plato nor Plotinus had heard Stochhausen's twelve-note bar, Schoenberg's noise, or Glass's silence.

Not all Modernist music is unpopular – Stravinsky's *La Mer* and *Rite of Spring* are played, and performed in public, quite often. So why doesn't the rest work? Of all the arts music is the one most likely to open up a sense of contact with Plato's Being. As always, the route is through beauty, and there is no other way, as we've seen. Music, like poetry, is a pretty strict pattern of sound and so it has to follow the patterns of notes, keys and scales which the West has found to be beautiful. Discordant noises and un-naturally patterned sounds just won't work, not for most Westerners. It disobeys the nature of things and so is bound to fail.

Throughout 2013, a century after the show in the Armory, the South Bank in London put on a year of modernist music. They had a website, *The Rest is Noise.* "Join us to explore how race, sex and politics shaped the most important music of the 20th century." And there in a sentence is the problem: art is to explore race, sex and politics. Art is now a sub-Marxist critique of society, with the intent to subvert and overthrow.

Sex, race and politics are epitomised by Conceptual Art, which is surprisingly long-lived, having begun in the 1960s and still not at an end. (It offers its practitioners too much to let it go so easily, perhaps.) In theory, Idea-art could work Platonically since concepts can be beautiful too. The idea, though, would have to be a good one and most (all?) conceptual artists seem pretty shallow. Shocking – or cocking a snook at – the middle classes isn't enough. To that end, we've had canned excreta (the artist's own, it said on the label), Christ in a beaker of urine (again the artist's own, so he said), pickled cows, unmade beds, a bust made of the sculptor's own blood, a box of flies, a box of a hundred microscope slides stained with the blood of a hundred poets (one poet per slide). This latter was created in the pre-DNA '60s – so is it really poets' and not pig's blood, or red ink? And does it matter? Would red ink turn it from a work of art to something fraudulent? And the 'concept' behind the blood letting? Poets give their life's blood for their work, like the martyr'd dead whose life's blood stained the *Red Flag*.

And what about Mrs Antin's boots? Ninety-six size tens, four size sixes, moving up and down the continental USA, mysteriously materialising in different places, sometimes walking in single file, sometimes in parade ground rows. At each stop, and at artistically correct intervals, black and white pictures were taken and posted to a thousand writers and artists. The boots themselves only became art when they turned up at MOMA in New York. 'Art is what's in an art gallery', 'art is anything an artist says it is', 'everybody is an artist'. The boots were Wellingtons, too: what would the Iron Duke have made of that? Too much money, not enough talent?

With the '60s and '70s also came Minimalism – a backlash, I understand, against Conceptualism. Minimalism is about matter, not ideas. A chalk circle was one work, a low wall of bricks (grey, I think) was another, along with bales of hay in a meadow, square pillars, and plastic blocks scattered randomly. Why don't these ideas work? Walls, for example, can be very evocative of Being, whether built of hand-sized Medieval brick, 18th century hand-made ones, or 19th century machine-made, industrially baked clay. Yet Carl Andre's *Bricks* (1976) didn't work and the reason, I think, is context. A brick wall in a remote village with a *Victoria Regina* post box set into it is evocative of time, peace and war, rain and passing summers. Bricks on a gallery floor can't evoke any such thing and the beauty is as much in evoked feelings – of sadness and repose – as in the texture and colour of the brick.

'Earth works', sculpture in a landscape, can work – mainly, I suspect, because landscape has the beauty needed for a lift-off back to Being. They can work as ideas, too: have to, in fact, because they don't usually last long and they're almost always in out of the way places. Walter de Maria's *The Lightning Field* (1977) works as an idea – in the sense that you can imagine it existing quietly on the semi-arid high plains beyond

Albuquerque in New Mexico, waiting for lightning. Four hundred steel rods stand upright in a grid measuring a mile by a kilometre. Each rod is roughly twenty feet high – they vary in length to take account of the unevenness of the ground, so the plane of their tips is perfectly flat. They're flexible and visible mainly in the morning or the evening light, and by the moon. The landscape is noted for its lightning strikes and each rod, of course, is a conductor. There are some beautiful photographs of great white jagged stalks of lightning striking them. But you don't need visual aids: just imagine it.

But if that is so, why go to the bother of finding the site, making the rods, hammering them into place? Why not just describe what you had in mind and let people imagine it? It's a beautiful idea – calling down lightning on the high plains, remote from eyes – which doesn't need matter to make real. Is that the flaw in Conceptual Art – not all ideas need illustrating because the physical work gets in the way of the idea?

Yet things are not always so well in the West. In 2012, three million books were published, one way or another, in the US alone. That's about one percent of the population. If, say, nine others were also at the pre-publication stage, it would mean around thirty million Americans are writing books at any one time. The population of England in 1600 was just under five million, among them Shakespeare and Donne. The population of England passed the thirty million mark somewhere between 1860 and 1870. Tennyson was in his fifties and had already written *In Memoriam.* Dickens had only two more novels to write – and a half, if you count *Edwin Drood.* It's conceivable that Eleanor Antin did find a hundred poets to give blood: there must be tens of thousands of them, none all that good, or any good.

Too often today, as we've said, the arts fail to do their job of expanding consciousness (they're better at shrinking it) yet for some people there seems to be nothing for consciousness to expand into: what they can experience is limited, it seems, and so they tend to drift into atheism, aided by the impossibility of logic ever reconciling itself to an un-Greek Creator God.

67

CHAPTER SEVEN

Counter-Consciousness

Not that there's anything new about atheism. Plato argued with fictionalised atheists in the *Laws*, a book about how to run an ideal city-state, in this case called Magnesia. His reasons for being against atheism are quite modern too: it was a problem because, without the gods, there could have been no absolute moral authority and, without that, people would have done what they liked. Even more astonishing is how little atheists have changed between the 4th century BC and the 21st AD. They'll put their case, said Plato, with ridicule, bantering and scorn. They still do. "Gentlemen", they'll say (said Plato), "prove the gods exist or we won't believe. Give us evidence or shut up." They still say that too – though instead of 'the gods' they say the 'Bronze Age sky fairy, or the imaginary friend of men in frocks'.

Even the same proofs are being bandied about. Cleinias said proof is easy to come by – look at the regularity of the heavens and the design of the universe. "No," Plato replied. "The bantering scoundrels will say the moon, the sun and the stars are just stones in the sky." Plato's own proof is, needless to say, also invalid. His argument is about movement. Things move. Things move things. Somewhere, therefore, something must give them a push and since that can't be matter it must be soul and soul is – he makes a terrific leap – the gods.

And even in Plato's day atheism wasn't new. In the 6th century BC Xenophanes seemed to think the gods were inventions: horses would invent horsey gods if they could invent anything. Protagoras, an older contemporary of Socrates, thought "Man is the measure of all things". You can't imagine the Cynics being particularly god-full (god-awful, perhaps). Cicero (106-43 BC) probably doubted that the gods existed yet he carried out the rituals believing they helped keep society together.

The creator God concept makes *logical* belief impossible – it can be held only by an act of faith, or through unreflectiveness. The Jews, whose idea it was, also seem to have had trouble with it: "The fool hath said in his heart 'there is no God'", for example, is from *Psalm 14* (possibly from the 10th/11th century BC), In the 11th century AD we find St Anselm, Archbishop of Canterbury, saying: 'credo ut intelligam' ('I believe in order to understand') which in turn is a variation on St Augustine's imperative 'crede, ut intelligas' ('believe in order to understand') from the 5th century AD. *They* believed but it must have been harder for others.

There were heretics, of course, but not ones you could call atheist. A few Amalricians were burned at the stake in Paris in the early 13th century but they were pantheists with no belief in the immortality of the soul. Later that same century, Siger of Brabant thought that the earth was not made by God but is eternal, and that nobody has an individual soul but each of us is only a cell in world-wide brain. This could be pantheist, of course, but he – and his followers – tempered it by saying faith taught that God was the creator. Both theories were right, they said. (Dante sent Siger, who was murdered, to Paradise.)

In the 14th century the Dutch monk, Ruysbroeck, divided people into two groups, each with a subdivision: in one set, Seers were out-and-out mystics, while Secret Friends were only mildly so. In the other set, Marthas were believers but with no personal access to what they believed in. Hirelings were only out for themselves and may well have harboured a few closet atheists in their ranks, Prelates and Princes of the Church included.

Atheism started to come out of the closet after the Scientific Revolution. Thomas Hobbes (1588-1679) – the first of the British Empiricists (if you overlook Occam and the two

Bacons) – was a materialist. His God, if he really believed in one, was made of matter which is all right for pantheists but not believers in a supernatural and immaterial Creator, although Tertullian (160-*c*.225 AD) thought of God as superfine, energy-like, matter (as is the soul) after the manner of the Stoics.

Newton worried that believing matter if freed from God would lead to atheism. In 1710, Bishop Berkeley (still only twenty-five and several years away from his bishopric) published his *Principles of Human Knowledge,* the subtitle of which tells it was an enquiry into the grounds of atheism, scepticism and irreligion. Three years later he wrote articles for Richard Steele's *Guardian* attacking free-thinkers, including atheists. Like Plato he was against materialism because it always ended in atheism and atheism could only end in social collapse, moral decay and physical poverty.

In the late 17th century, atheism, it seems, was still something to hide. Jean Meslier (1664-1729), a village priest in Northern France, was a materialist, an atheist and a communist (of the non-Marxist kind of course) but he kept it all to himself: his works were printed only after he died. Later in the 18th century, Baron d'Holbach, the Franco-German *philosophe,* was open enough to lay out the case for materialism and atheism in Diderot's *Encyclopedia:* the supernatural, he argued, is not needed to explain the movement of matter and, besides, religion erases morals. (The Deistic Voltaire was scandalised.)

Not everybody admitted to atheism, even later in the century – David Hume (1711-1776) didn't, though it's thought he was. Schelling (1775-1854) condemned atheists as philistines blind to the beauty of tradition and ritual. But Schelling's contemporary, Schopenhauer (1788-1860), was openly atheist, while in the 1880s, Nietzsche killed God because Christianity had abandoned its Greek origins and opted for the weakness of a slave mentality. In England in the 1880s, Charles Bradlaugh (1833-1891), one-time Sunday School teacher, Dragoon and MP, was behind a change in the law on the taking of oaths to allow atheistic affirmation in place of swearing on the Bible. (In 1866 he'd co-founded the National Secular Society.) Almost exactly a hundred years later, Don Cupitt, an Anglican priest, wrote *Taking Leave of God*. Out of it came the Sea of Faith movement. "God is the sum of our values," Cupitt wrote in explanation, echoing Protagoras. 19th century England was full of atheists though they were balanced by the mystically inclined. The Church of England, for example, sent missionaries on to public works to convert the heathen navvies, usually unsuccessfully. In 1874 Lord Salisbury said: "A good deal of the political battle of the future will be a conflict between religion and unbelief, and women will in that controversy be on the right side." Fourteen years later at a meeting of the Primrose League he supported suffrage because he believed women would vote "in the direction of morality and religion." He was right about belief, wrong about women. Today atheists are commonplace: you can read extremely long lists of them on the Web, broken down into professions. (The Church isn't there, but it could be.) Some are missionaries out to convert people to infidelity, or to fidelity to infidelity.

Again, there's nothing new in preaching the gospel of atheism. Berkeley wrote *Alciphron* (1732) in Colonial Rhode Island while waiting for the Government to help him set up a college in Bermuda to train his missionaries. The book is about freethinking atheists of a type Plato would have recognised. "To speak the Truth, (freethinking) has given them a certain Air and Manner, which a little too visibly declare they think themselves wiser than the rest of the World". Alciphron is one of the Freethinkers whose freedom of thought has turned him into an atheist because none of the world's religions can agree on what God is or even if there is one – which has a rather modern ring: "*you* find the reasons and I'll believe them". Waiting for others to convince him doesn't stop his preening: "Atheism therefore, that Bugbear of Women and Fools, is the very Top and Perfection of Freethinking." True genius, he goes on, naturally rises to it whereas the Vulgar have been brainwashed and are kept in line by the eye of the Magistrate and the eyes of the priest and his God. Religion is a "Confederacy," says Lysicles, "between the Prince and the Priesthood to subdue the People". In allowing this, we have "lost our Liberty and Property", and people have bought "Bridles and Saddles for their own Backs". Bringing down the system, changing society, was already the aim of atheists in the 1730s, at least according to Berkeley who (about to become a Bishop) was of course biased against them. The political and religious system was already being brought slowly down, says Alciphron. Prejudice against atheism "lessens every day among the better sort; and when it is quite worn out, our Free-thinkers may then (and not till then) be said to have given the finishing Stroke to Religion." Once the root is gone, the shoots will perish too and with them 'Notions of Conscience, Duty, Principle, and the like, which fill a Man's Head with Scruples, awe him with Fears, and make him a more thorough Slave than the Horse he rides."

The astonished Euphranor tells Alciphron that the Gentlemen of his Sect are 'admirable Weeders' who have 'rooted up a World of Notions." But what will you put in their place?

The "Appetites, Passions and Senses" will be set free, says Alciphron instantly. "Food, Drink, Sleep, and the like animal Enjoyments being what all Men like and love."

Euphranor – the believer – then appeals to Cicero who said he'd be sorry to know the truth if those who denied immortality were right. Furthermore, said Cicero, I acknowledge "no sort of Obligation" to believe the people who think that way. Cicero also had a name for people like you, Euphranor tells Alciphron – the Minute Philosophers. This fits freethinkers and atheists because they are a "sort of Sect which diminish all the most valuable things, the Thoughts, Views, and Hopes of Men: all the Knowledge, Notions and Theories of the Mind they reduce to Sense; Human Nature they contract and degrade to the narrow low

Standard of Animal Life, and assign us only a small Pittance of Time instead of Immortality." (They shrink consciousness, in other words.)

Like the atheists of Plato's time, and those of today, Alciphron is smugly unshakeable. Yes, he says, we *are* Minute Philosophers but not for Cicero's reasons: *we* consider things "minutely, not swallowing them in the gross, as other Men are used to. Besides we all know the best Eyes are necessary to discern the minutest Objects. It seems therefore, that Minute Philosophers might have been so called from their Distinguished Perspicacity."

No, says Euphranor. "These Minute Philosophers are a sort of Pirates who plunder all that come their way. I consider myself as a Man left stripped and desolate on a bleak beach."

There was a real Alciphron in the 2nd century AD (probably) who wrote in the Attic dialect of the 4th century BC. He wrote letters from the point of view of farmers or fishermen, all with an erotic tinge. Berkeley's Alciphron, on the other hand, is said to have been based on the 3rd Earl of Shaftesbury, a kind of semi-Platonist in that he associated morals with beauty but not the eternal Forms which are lodged in Being. He also argued for intuitive or creative reasoning against the drier analytical kind. (As such he influenced German Idealists like Schelling and Hagel and so, ultimately, Marx – the Law of Unintended Consequences at work.) Berkeley apparently thought of Shaftesbury as a deist with little of religion about him.

Berkeley's Lysicles, the more hard line atheist, is said to have been based on Bernard Mandeville, the Dutchman who scandalised people with his opinions. Lysicles justifies the overthrowing of society through a philosophy based on the nature of things – the passions and appetites are natural and therefore have to be indulged. (The Sophists said the same thing in the days of Socrates.) Vice, crime and self-harming behaviour, says Lysiclces/Mandeville, is good for the economy. Behind every drunk, for example, are a host of tradesmen – all earning and circulating money – from brewers and maltsters (the Malt Tax alone keep other taxes down) to smiths and carpenters. Throw in the wine drinkers and you need shipwrights and sailors, sail-makers and victualers. Suppose a Man of mean birth ruins a Man of breeding who then turns highwayman, doesn't the money still go round? Doesn't the robber spend the money he's stolen? His merry life is short and ends with the payment of a reward to whoever turns him in.

Two hundred and seventy years after *Alciphron* the system hasn't quite toppled but people are still trying it give it a shove and they're much closer to winning outright – the shoots are perishing one by one. Two books by latter-day Alciphrons and Lysicles can stand in for them all – they're all much of a muchness: Richard Dawkins's *The God Delusion* (2006) and Christopher Hitchens's *god is not Great* (2007). Two recurring ideas are central to their arguments – somebody else has to prove the existence of God because it's not up to them to disprove it (which often sounds petulant) and organised religion has done bad things (which often sounds sulky).

Of those two points all we can say is:

1. There are no proofs of God's existence. None whatsoever.

2. Almost everything they say about religion is true. To modern eyes its history has been appalling – wars, burnings at the stake, torture, cruelty of all kinds. Yet the fault must be in human nature because there is nothing in Christianity which urges people to violence. "So", says Alciphron, "we're not longer to blame Christians for the cruelty of the Inquisition?" "Oh, yes," says Crito, "blame Christians all you like, but not Christianity. If a Believer doth Evil, it is owing to the Man, not his Belief. And if an Infidel doth Good, it is owing to the Man, and not his Infidelity." But Berkeley hadn't come across a creed where evil is part of the belief – there was an innocence about some aspects of the past we can no longer conceive.

74

But what atheists did (and do) is cherry-pick a sub-section of a subsection of the religious market (Christianity only) and call it the whole: only concrete, exoteric, communal, ritualised religion as organised in churches is looked at. In two thousand years, bad things are bound to have mounted up and the atheists go only for the bad end of the spectrum, not the good. As with so many things, this is nothing new. The 17th century Divine, Joseph Hall (1574-1656), who had been a bishop until Cromwell's victory in the Civil Wars, likened the cherry-pickers to flies gathering on the sores of a horse. "How these flies swarm to the galled part of this poor beast; and there sit, feeding upon that worst part of his skin! It must," he added, "needs be a filthy creature that feeds upon nothing but corruption."

Like all religions, atheism needs its great men, and sometimes facts have to be twisted to fit the narrative. Martin Luther King, Hitchens wrote, wasn't a Christian because he forgave people. This in spite of millions of people asking, daily in the Lord's Prayer, for the strength to forgive those who trespass against them and Christ's "Father, forgive them for they know not what they do" spoken from the Cross itself. For Dawkins, Mendel couldn't have been a proper monk because he was a scientist, as though getting taken on in a 19th century monastery was like gaining a research grant in one of the better universities. To get in, to prove he had a vocation, Mendel must have lied and cheated. "Newton did indeed claim to be religious." Pope John Paul II was a hypocrite for saying he believed in Darwinism, something reserved for scientists and atheists, perhaps. Presumably the Pope was lying too.

Hitchens was a Trotskyist until that ideology let him down but, as he said, "what else was to be expected of something that was produced by the close cousins of chimpanzees?" (Isn't atheism also the product of the chimp's cousin?) His book is in parts a missionary tract: "Thus, dear reader, if you have come this far and found your own faith undermined – as I hope – I am willing to say that to some extent I know what you are going through. There are days when I miss my old convictions as if they were an amputated limb. But in general I feel better, and no less radical, and you will feel better too, I guarantee, once you leave hold of the doctrinaire and allow your chainless mind to do its own thinking."

Most books have their errors. Hitchens was wrong about Occam. When Occam said the stars don't have to exist physically, he didn't mean what we might mean: he had no concept of light years or the speed of light and that, therefore, we might be seeing photons from a star which blew up aeons ago and is no longer physically in place: he meant God can put an image in the eye without the physical object being there. Both Hitchens and Dawkins were wrong about the Greeks not being monotheists. Socrates was, as well as being a polytheist and a part time agnostic. Plato's The Good evolved into a monotheistic god. The Stoics were pantheists and so their one god was everything: it was pure material intelligence. Zeus wasn't a Creator – the Greeks had no concept of a Creator God in the Judaic sense: Plato's Demiurge shaped pre-existing energy into triangular atoms – equilateral, isosceles and scalene – out of which he then made earth, fire, air and water and then, once he'd made the gods, he got them to make bodies – animals and people – but not human souls. (To be pedantically accurate, there's one brief reference in *The Republic* to an over-all maker who, Plato tells us, is hard to discover, impossible to explain.) There was no linear evolution in the Greek world from polytheism to monotheism: at any one time, there were polytheists, monotheists, atheists, pantheists, hylozoists, mystics and materialists all mingling together. Pletho, one of the scholars who brought Greek learning to Renaissance Italy, was a polytheist. Christianity wasn't spread through the Roman Empire by force. The Crusades were to recover Christian lands lost to Islamic imperialism. Christianity was taken to the world outside Europe only partly by soldiers. Who in the British Empire was converted by force? Nobody in India.

Christopher Hitchens's assault on Christianity was countered by his brother, Peter, in *The Rage Against God.* Christopher said, for example, that the command to 'love thy neighbour as thy thyself' is unfeasible: nobody cares for another as they care for themselves. Not true, said Peter, listing mothers and their children, doctors in epidemics, soldiers in battle, husbands caring for bed-bound, incontinent and demented wives (and vice versa he could have added). Without the Christian code anchored in the authority of God, he said (unwittingly repeating Plato), these bonds would weaken and, with them, so would society (and that, in fact is what is happening). In support of his argument he wrote a whole chapter on the Soviet Union's dedication to the destruction of Greek Orthodoxy and the degradation it brought about. (He also had a lot to say about the Webbs and other pre-War fellow travellers.)

Both Christopher Hitchens and Dawkins could have made more of evolution theory. Why, Hitchens asked, did Christ appear when he did and not earlier? C H Dodd had already answered that one – people had evolved to a point where they could take in new ideas. Why, Hitchens asked, did the Old Testament have no hell, while the New did? Because the authors of the Old Testament never evolved a concept of life after death at all: that was a Greek idea, taken over by later Judaism. Then the hell idea evolved further. By the early 3rd century, Origen taught that in time everybody, Satan included, would be saved and hell would be shut down. That was deemed heretical but at least the idea had evolved – Christianity is an evolutionary religion.

Dawkins was wrong about mystics – they don't "exult in mystery and want it to stay mysterious. Scientists exult in mystery for a different reason: it gives them something to do." This is a running together of two kinds of mystery. What mystics see is not (at the time) a mystery but incomparable clarity, a reconnection with something which seems so right as to be completely un-mysterious. 'Mystery' is the wrong word entirely to apply to mystics – the etymology's the same but little else. And scientists surely don't do science to fill in the emptiness of their lives. Do they?

Why do people believe in God? Dawkins had three reasons. To begin with he blamed it on the programmability of children: their parents, themselves cruelly pre-programmed, programme them with their own misguided misbeliefs, and it shouldn't be allowed (what did Hume, another atheist (probably) say: "you can't get an 'ought' from an 'is'?). Instead, children should be programmed to think for themselves, presumably, that is, like atheists. In his book *Siris,* Bishop Berkeley explained away the common belief in the existence of matter in a similar way: everybody is steeped in matter from the earliest age and so material things "amuse the eyes and ears, and are more suited to vulgar uses and the mechanic arts of life" and so we come to see matter as primary even though, as Wordsworth pointed out, we enter the world 'trailing clouds of glory'.

Children are dualists, runs Dawkins's second reason why people are theists, who think quite naturally that mind and matter are separate. They're also born thinking that the things of the world have a purpose – a sharp rock is a scratching post for handless animals. Dualism easily leads to belief in a soul while the child's teleological bias tells her that the world has a purpose and that purpose is, the priest tells her, God's.

Love, Dawkins went on with his third reason, offers the species an evolutionary advantage because it encourages child care. The cause of this love is a 'neurally active drug' which occurs naturally in the brain. The same drug also activates a love of God to give people a warm feeling of protection in a mechanical world. Religion is the outcome of these two facts combined.

What it all might mean, of course, is that neither Hitchens (Christopher) nor Dawkins had access to the Platonist strand of consciousness. While below all this seems to lie the fear that Christian fundamentalism will win and then ban science. Harmless, non-fundamental, brands of religion clear the way for the fundamentalist kind and so have to also go. In 2006 Dawkins worried that the US was becoming a theocracy: two years later, other people worried the US was becoming a socialist welfare state and the odds are they were right and Dawkins and his fears were wrong.

Dawkins told a story about a little girl's imaginary friend. One day the friend said goodbye: he'd be back only when she really needed him. Years later she did: he re-appeared pushing a heap of books towards her as a sign for her to go to university. Dawkins wept, and very nearly understood how *ordinary* people find consolation in gods. (This hasn't been made up though 'almost wept' or 'nearly became tearful' might be slightly more accurate.)

Why are there so many atheists these days? In his book *The Last Word,* Thomas Nagel, professor of philosophy in New York University, was open about it: "I want atheism to be true and am made uneasy by the fact that some of the most intelligent and well-informed people I know are religious believers. It isn't just that I don't believe in God and, naturally, hope that I'm right in my belief. It's that I hope there is no God! I don't want there to be a God; I don't want the universe to be like that... My guess is that this cosmic authority problem is not a rare condition and that it is responsible for much of the scientism and reductionism of our time. One of the tendencies it supports is the ludicrous overuse of evolutionary biology to explain everything about life, including everything about the human mind."

In a debate in the mid-90s, the geneticist Richard Lewontin also came clean: "We take the side of science in spite of the patent absurdity of some of its constructs, in spite of its failure to fulfil many of its extravagant promises of health and life, in spite of the tolerance of the scientific community for unsubstantiated just-so stories, because we have a prior commitment to materialism." It isn't the scientific method which comes up with materialist results – those results are pre-ordained by the materialist mindset of the scientist. 'We cannot allow a Divine Foot in the door."

In England, more so than in the US, the Left have another reason for wanting to uproot Christianity. "But what is it that they have against the Christian God?" Peter Hitchens asked, and replied: "He is their chief rival. Christian belief, by subjecting all men to divine authority and by asserting in the words 'My Kingdom is not of this world' that the ideal society does not exist in this life, is the most coherent and potent obstacle to secular utopianism. Christ's reproof of Judas – 'the poor always ye have with you' – is also a stumbling-block and an annoyance to world reformers. By putting such socialistic thoughts in the mouth of the despised traitor-to-be Judas, and by stating so baldly the truth known to all conservatives that poverty cannot be eradicated, the Bible angers and frustrates those who believe that the pursuit of a perfect society justifies the quest for absolute power."

In the end, all this is the to-be-expected result of a shrunken consciousness. In *Mysticism in Religion,* Dean Inge spoke about Personal Platonism, an idea of a man called J A Stewart. Personal Platonism is "the mood of one who has a curious eye for the endless variety of this visible and temporal world, and a fine sense of its beauties, yet is haunted by the presence of an invisible and eternal world behind." That immaterial world beyond is closed to millions of materialists today, even though the concept of immateriality in the West is a good two and a half thousand years old.

CHAPTER EIGHT

Immateriality Isn't Immaterial

Like most things in the West, the idea of immateriality began with the Greeks. Plato (429-347 BC) was the first to confound materialists by simply pointing out that ideas are immaterial. But he wasn't the first to realise that things can be asomatic, bodiless, intangible, incorporeal, non-physical and still exist. The idea of immateriality is *implicit* in both Anaximander (611-564 BC) and his younger contemporary Anixemenes (580-528 BC) both of whom said the cosmos is run by laws or rules, which are (by definition) immaterial. The concept of immateriality *may* have become *explicit* in the work of Anaxagoras (c.500-428 BC). Diogenes Laertius said: "He was the first to set Mind above Matter". Anaxagoras was a pre-Socratic (just – his life overlapped that of Socrates and he died when Plato was around one year old). He was interested in rainbows, meteors, meteorites and eclipses. To him, the sun was a blazing rock, torn from the earth's side, no bigger than the Peloponnese. Moonlight is reflected sunlight. The moon has mountains and mountaineers. He was a friend of Euripides and Pericles, not that that saved him when the Athenians turned against him, accusing him either of impiety or starting the Peloponnesian War.

A monument to Mind was erected at Lampsacus in the Dardanelles in memory of Anaxagoras. Mind was all-knowing, all-powerful and was possibly also the soul. Mind/soul are the cause of beauty and order, which go together. The only doubt is – was his Mind immaterial, as some say? In the *Phaedo,* Socrates tells us that as a young man he read Anaxagoras but gave up because the old philosopher hadn't gone far enough. Why did Mind do what it did? What is the purpose of it all? Also, it seems, Socrates dismissed him when he realised that the Anaxagoran Mind was in fact made up of matter.

Whatever the truth, it's certain that the *explicit* idea of immateriality dates from 5th century BC Athens and that Socrates was in at the beginning. It's been a world-changing idea and the men of genius behind it are Socrates and Plato, the West's real and un-mythical founders (along with Aristotle).

W K C Guthrie in his book, *Socrates,* wrote: "To sum up, Socrates believed in a god who was the supreme Mind, responsible for the ordering of the universe and at the same time the creator of men. Men moreover had a special relation with him in that their own minds, which controlled their bodies as God controlled the physical movements of the universe, were, though less perfect than the mind of God, of the same nature, and worked on the same principles. In fact, if one looked only to *arete* of the human soul and disregarded its shortcomings, the two were identical. Whether or not because of this relationship, God had a special regard for man, and had designed both man's own body and the rest of nature for his benefit." In other words, the apex of the human soul is also divine.

Plato (and possibly Socrates) was influenced by Pythagoras (a spiritual philosopher) and by Orphism (a mystical religion) – but the higher world of both was still a physical one. Socrates's God was not. Nor probably were the gods he also believed in – they were, more likely, incorporeal forces of nature. Socrates also gave the West its idea of soul. The Christian soul is Socratic. In the *Phaedo*, Plato has Socrates give his reasons for believing in the soul's immortality: the best argument (they're all weak): 'what has no parts can't die and the soul is supremely simple'. The immaterial idea of being – of existence itself – indicates eternity and therefore the absence of death.

5th century BC Athens turned to humanism away from the uncertainty of Pre-Socratic science. Sophistry and Socratism were the main competing schools, as far as we're concerned.

Like post-modernists, Sophists were relativists. You have to live by the laws of nature, they argued, so man-made laws can be disobeyed when it's to your advantage to do so. Words like justice, courage, excellence were just that – words with multiple meanings which change with place and time.

Socrates disagreed: he believed in an absolute truth which we need to know in order to answer correctly that primary and vital question: how should be live? There had to be a fixed but immaterial reality behind and beyond words otherwise they're meaningless: you can't act justly unless you know what justice is. (Justice is what the powerful say it is, said the Sophists.) Socrates wasn't preaching a doctrine but trying to show how little we know and therefore the need to go on looking.

But first you have to find it. What is the good or virtue, exactly? To live by it, you must know it. We talk of single virtues (justice, courage, temperance, holiness and wisdom) but they must be aspects of a deep single abstraction – the Good – which, if we could contact it, would make us live our lives properly and without wrong doing (we do wrong out of ignorance of the right) or damaging our invisible souls. Virtue is needed for the health and well-being of the soul, and life with a ruined soul isn't worth living. Finding that single Master-Good was Socrates's life's work. To look for it, he invented, or discovered, logic, inductive reasoning, the need to define words precisely, dialectics and *elenchus,* all of which come together in what is still called the Socratic Method. Begin with a proposition, question its truth and prove it false: then take the next proposition and repeat. Any false reasoning in the chain, Plato realised, invalidates the whole argument – a kind of pre-Popper falsification theory, and a nice irony given Popper's contempt for the old Greek philosopher whose spirituality I don't think he understood.

Elenchus means refuting a proposition with logic. We have the word in the hybrid Latin-Greek phrase *ignoratio elenchi* – the fallacy of refuting something which has not been said. (The best example is Dr Johnson's kicking of a stone to prove

Berkeley wrong although – as we'll see – the Bishop didn't say what Johnson said he said.) As an example of the Socratic Methods we'll take the *Hippias Major* even though it's uncertain whether it's by Plato or not (it's different from every other Dialogue – lighter and funnier) but it's short (usually under thirty printed pages) and the virtue being examined is *to kalon* – beauty – which is the connecting rod between heaven and earth.

Hippias was a rich man who made his money through Sophistry. He was an itinerant lecturer in rhetoric and public speaking who taught wealthy young men how to argue eristically to win, not dialectically, as Socrates did, to find the truth. He also taught maths, memory training (he could himself memorise fifty names after one hearing), history, astronomy and – more surprisingly – ethics. *Kalos* in Plato's Attic Greek meant 'fine, noble, admirable' as well as beautiful. (In modern Greek, it still means good, noble and so on while 'beautiful' is now *omorphos*.) In the introduction to his translation of the *Hippias Major*, Paul Woodruff said *kalos* could be applied to "sound laws and good habits, fast horses and fierce fighting birds." A soldier could be *kalos* as an officer in the field, *kakos* as a man. Throughout his translation, Woodruff translated *to kalon* as 'fine'.

The question around which the *Hippias Major* revolves is: "What is the ultimate essence of fineness without which nothing can fine?" What is the abstract quality which makes all beautiful things beautiful? (And, by extension, makes piety pious, justice just and so on.)

A fine girl is a fine/beautiful thing, Hippias first answered. Mares bred in my native Elis are beautiful/fine.

So, asked Socrates, is a well-thrown pot (particularly a two-handled one holding six *choes*) fine or beautiful? Hippias baulked at the vulgarity of that. It isn't in the same league as girls and horses, he replied.

Socrates then quoted Heraclitus – is a monkey beautiful when set beside something uglier? If that's true, wouldn't even the most beautiful girl be ugly alongside a god? That's sacrilege, objected Hippias

But we're missing the point, Socrates started again. There must be an essence of fineness in all fine things. Some one thing must make all beauty beautiful, some hidden common factor. What is it?

Then, possibly for the first time (and possibly not), beauty is called a Form, Eidos, Idea (or an Abstraction).

The dialectical questioning and answering went on until Hippias snapped in exasperation: 'everything beautiful is gold'.

So, said Socrates, why did Pheidias make the statue of Athena (in the Parthenon) out of ivory with stone eyes? Is stone beautiful?

Depends what it's used for, Hippias answered.

Well, said Socrates, would you rather stir a pot of bean soup with a spoon made out of figwood or out of gold?

I see, said Hippias, that you're looking for something to explain why beautiful things can never be seen as foul at any time or anywhere.

The next proposition was that the fine or beautiful is what is useful. But bad workmanship can be useful at times. Ableness and unableness didn't work out either. Beautiful is the beneficial? But then 'the beneficial is the maker of the good. The maker is thus the cause but the cause is then different from what it's the cause of'.

Is the beautiful simply that which delights us through sight or hearing? After a lot of backing and forthing that too fell down.

Hippias had made more money out of selling wisdom than any man alive: Socrates had made nothing – which proved, said Socrates ironically, that Hippias must be the wiser of two. So what, Hippias, is the one single in-common attribute underlying all things fine/beautiful/noble/admirable?

Finally, an impatient Hippias dismissed Socrates as a reductionist. What is beautiful is beautiful as a whole. Making money out of making a speech which gets you all the prizes – that's fine, noble and beautiful.

In the end, neither knew what was the essence of beauty. Socrates ended by quoting a proverb: "what is *to kalon* is hard". But it wouldn't be so hard, he might have added, if we'd uncovered the essence of Virtue, and isolated the Good. He never did find the answer to any of his questions (nor has anybody else) but it didn't matter too much. *Know Thyself* and *the unexamined life is not worth living* have become the other Socratic maxims (though 'know yourself was Apollo's reminder to people that they are far from being gods and should act accordingly). At the end of the dialectic ordeal, the people involved should know that they know nothing – which is the beginning of wisdom and inward transformation, though not for Hippias. But also they should know that there's more to life than matter, that the most deeply motivating things are immaterial. (In the end, Plato came to realise that you can 'see' these immaterial ideas mystically but not through reason: in other words, through the Platonist strand of consciousness.)

Nor did Socrates ever say where these abstractions are located – except to note they have their own existence outside the mind. Plato however took over the concept, called them Ideas, Forms or Eidoi, and placed them in an eternal and unchanging realm called Being (in time the Christian Heaven). But Being on its own is incomplete, as impossible as a one-ended piece of string. To be complete, Being needs to be balanced by Becoming, the material world of corruption and corrosion. (Erigena picked up the idea in the 9th century. God had to create the world to balance His own perfection with imperfection. To be complete, even the Absolute needs the non-absolute.)

A Platonic Form or Idea (or Abstraction) is not unlike 'idea' as we use the word in English today. Plotinus, in the 3rd century AD, put it nicely: a beautiful house is "an idea stamped on stone." Beautiful the house may be but, as Plato said, everything down here is but a poor decaying material copy of what's eternal, pure and perfect. Perhaps a Form is a distillation of the best that could, but never will, be. Eyes can't see them, mind can. In the end Plato came to see what-can't-be-seen as divine and the Form of the Good as a kind of God. Plato said no more about the Forms or tried to explain or describe them, because they are beyond speech and thought: they can occasionally be experienced, never described.

More prosaically, Aristotle said the Forms came logically out of the puzzle of how you can have stability in a cosmos in constant flux as Heraclitus argued. In the *Metaphysics* Aristotle said: "When Socrates was busying himself with ethical questions (to the complete neglect of nature as a whole) and was seeking in them for the universal and directing the mind for the first time to definitions, Plato, accepting his teaching, came to the conclusion that it applied to something other than the sensible world: the common definition, he reasoned, could not apply to any of the sensibles, since they were always changing."

But Aristotle was probably only partly right: there was another side to Plato, if not to Socrates, which can't be ignored, though today it usually is. Few of the few people writing about Plato nowadays want to believe that he was a mystic, yet there's little doubt that he was. In his book, *The Greek Philosophers,* Guthrie wrote: "Platonism is undoubtedly a two-world philosophy, and anyone whose thoughts are confined to this world can never hope to understand it. Yet equally it is a closed book to him who is not alive to earthly beauty, which must be to the philosopher as the first rungs of the ladder which will finally take him all the way from bodily beauty to beauty in his ways, from there to the beauty of scholarship, and from there to the wondrous vision of beauty itself, never changing nor growing nor diminishing, nor yet beautiful in one part and not in another, but beauty itself, stripped of all fleshly colour and moral dross and standing out in the immortal radiance in which beauty and truth become one."

Authorship of the *Seventh Letter* is, again, disputed. All the same, if not by Plato it must have been written by somebody

87

who knew him. Most of it is about Plato's trips to Syracuse (another long story) but a short passage is clearly mystical. Only a few could grasp this philosophy, the writer said, but when they did, a spark would leap through the darkness to light a fire in their minds which could never be entirely put out. You have to find this out for yourself – it can't be taught. Nor should it be written down: reading about it could make some people believe they'd mastered a deep secret, giving them an unjustified contempt for others.

The Divided Line, I think, is also an analogy. Imagine a vertical line divided into two divisions and two sub-divisions. The bottom-most is like looking at the reflection of a coffee cup in the polished granite of a coffee shop table. Lift your eyes slightly and you see the real thing. So too with the upper division, the lower half of which is an 'intimation of immortality', but raise your inner eyes and you'll see the real thing – the realm of Being, the place of the Forms, the heaven to which the upper part of your soul wants to get back to.

On top of that, the cave myth is also clearly mystical – though some today argue it's about the effect on the mind of higher education, which is a bit vainglorious if you think you're highly educated, as those who make the claim do. In the cave, people sit chained, unable to move their heads, forced to stare at shadows moving across the rock wall. The shadows are of people and animals, often carrying things, moving along a walkway in front of a great fire. To the people in chains, these dim, blurred shadows are the real world. Only a very few can break away, climb up into the sunlight, and see the truth for themselves in a world of sunlit splendour. When they go back down again into the dark, those marooned there will jeer and scoff if told about it, and they still do. (That has to be qualified, of course: Ruysbroeck's Marthas believe there's light above the rock without ever experiencing it for themselves.)

Socrates explained the cave myth more fully to Glaucon in *The Republic*. "The visible realm should be likened to the prison dwelling, and the light of the fire inside it to the power of the sun. And if you interpret the upward journey and the study of the things above as the upward journey of the soul to the intelligible realm, you'll grasp what I hope to convey, since that is what you wanted to hear about. Whether it's true or not, only the god knows. But this is how I see it: in the knowable realm, the Form of the Good is the last thing to be seen, and it is reached only with difficulty. Once one has seen it, however, one must conclude that it is the cause of all that is correct and beautiful in anything, that it produces both light and its source in the visible realm, and that in the intelligible realm it it controls and provides truth and understanding, so that anyone who is to act sensibly in private or public must see it." (Grube's and Reeve's translation.)

The Good is like the sun which is neither sight nor the eye but which illuminates the truth and so lets sight and eye see it, and is itself the Truth. People who see by it want to go on doing so, and that – thought Plato – is a problem: they're needed to run the perfect City State as outlined in the *Republic:* they should be the Guardians of Kallipolis, the Good City, which is also the soul.

The Symposium clinches the case for Plato's mysticism. Each guest at a banquet gave his idea about love and what it is. Socrates repeated an explanation given him by a priestess called Diotima. Love is consciousness of the Form of Beauty and the Good. Love is the desire for them, the looking for them. Physical love between a man and woman (for procreation) is the lowest rung. Next comes the beauty of art, then the beauty of order, then of rules and laws, then of ideas. The attraction between men and teenage boys – as long as nothing physical happens – is higher still: it's about 'spiritual parenthood', unlike the lower kind.

Plato outlawed pederasty in both of his imaginary city-states, Magnesia in the *Laws* and Kallipolis in *The Republic.* What we now sometimes call Platonic attraction can lead the soul to Beauty because Eros is spiritual and the god can take you from love of beauty in a body to love of beauty of all kinds, including that of character and science, and then beyond the earthly to the Beauty of the eternal Forms or Abstractions, something only the eye of the soul can see. The mystic vision is what makes life worthwhile – "if the love of human beauty overwhelms us, what shall be the power of the love caused by Transcendent Beauty?"

Socrates was more practical and concrete than Plato, less – if at all – mystical. This is borne out also in *The Symposium* when Diotima doubted that Socrates could reach the highest level. On the other hand, in the *Phaedo* Socrates asked: "When does the soul attain truth?" When the mind is free of worldly things: in that state, and in that state alone, you can see the essence of Goodness, and absolute justice and beauty. (That, however, may just have been Plato the ventriloquist speaking.)

But only philosophers can see Being in all its beauty (in fact, Being and Beauty are one and the same) but even they need help. For newly joined recruits in Plato's Academy – a kind of university which lasted for over eight hundred years – maths and geometry were major subjects, their beauty and elegance being the easiest way to become aware of the Transcendent. Next came dialectics, usually between two people: a thesis was given – 'justice is teachable', perhaps – which they then chipped away at using the Socratic Method. The idea was to achieve self transformation, a rising above the self, and not to get at a truth which is always out of reach.

Other spiritual exercises were mind calming, contemplation and reminding yourself that, since you don't know what is really good or bad, getting yourself worked up won't help you or anybody else at all. Also ask yourself: How much does human life *really* matter? Socrates, also in the *Phaedo,* says that philosophy is a way of getting ready for death: when you die, body and soul split – so practise separating them beforehand. The purpose of physical sight is to see the mystical nature of things through looking at beautiful things, particular the heavens because the super-lunar realm is already perfect: souls released from reincarnation dwell there, each soul to its own star. So too with hearing – music is to restore the harmony of the soul.

Expand yourself, Plato advised like every mystic who has ever lived, until you become Cosmos: 'Become Cosmos' could have been the motto of Plato's Academy. The soul must lift itself above the worldly to contemplate the divine. The result could be a beatific vision of the Eleusinian or Orphic kind. As Victor Goldschmidt said: Plato wrote not to 'inform' as in 'tell' but to 'inform' as in 'shape'.

The Academy was not academic in the modern sense. Whitehead said: "The idea of pure knowledge, or pure understanding, was completely foreign to Plato's thoughts. The age of the Professors had not yet come." Yet Platonism still comes naturally to some people: (Leibnitz (1646-1716), for example, wanted to make a system out of the disparate bits of Plato's twenty-odd books. It also came naturally, I suggest, to some people long before Plato was born: Sappho, for example.

CHAPTER NINE

A Pre-Plato Platonist

When Socrates was walking to the courthouse in Athens to be tried for impiety, he met Euthyphro, a pious man, who was on his way to charge his own father with manslaughter. How pious was that? For half an hour or so they debated the essence of piety, inconclusively, as ever. All the same, as Gregory Vlastos pointed out, Socrates based his whole life on piety: in helping others he believed he was doing God's work on earth and if piety has any meaning at all, that surely is it?

Similarly, people who know nothing of Plato can live by contacting Being, even if they're materialists. Sappho, a 7th century BC Ionian, was one by definition – by definition because immateriality hadn't been thought of in her day. She even had her own idea of what beauty is – 'the beautiful is what you love best'. Beauty for her, she told us in a poem, didn't lie in regiments of cavalry manoeuvring in the sun, or warships at sea, but in the radiant eyes of her friend or lover, Anactoria, and in her gracefulness.

Not much is known about Sappho, even her birth date is uncertain – 650 BC? 630? flourished 600 BC? Certainly she lived in the 7th century, still the Archaic period but after the decline of the warrior clans of Homer and at the beginning of the city states. She was educated, aristocratic and may have been caught up in the politics of Lesbos, her native island. (She may have been exiled in the Greek colonies in Sicily for a time.) Probably she had a daughter, Cleis, and at least one brother. She is also one of the world's great poets – that's clear enough even though only fragments of her nine books have come down to us. In the fragments, and presumably in the rest of her work, her main (but not only) theme was love, particularly the love of a woman for a woman.

This of course scandalised later generations. Some argued that, if she'd been writing about physical love, she'd have scandalised people in her own time, men in particular, and so, therefore, Sappho was heterosexual. A legend grew up to prove it. Sappho, it was said, fell in love with Phaon, a ferryman, but, her love being unreturned, she threw herself off the Leucadian cliffs to her death. Phaon, however, was mythical – so mythical, in fact, that he ferried Aphrodite without a fee and she, in turn, changed him into a handsome young man, a kind of Adonis of the sea.

What Sappho really got up to, nobody knows. In her fragments, she reads like a kindly lady – motherly in places. She wrote (and probably sang) songs for weddings. Possibly she taught girls. Perhaps she was part of a circle of women devoted to the female gods. Certainly she was attached to Aphrodite, the goddess of love and beauty. But Aphrodite was from the south, from Cyprus, and a goddess of unfettered untameable love rather than the domestic wifely kind. Eros, her son, lives on in the English word 'erotic' of course.

Sappho inspired the Greek-speaking Callimachus and the Latin-speaking Catullus – that 1st century BC prototype of the Earl of Rochester, the Restoration's rhyming pornographer. Ovid was drawn to her since he also wrote about *amor*. Naturally she almost vanished in the dark Christian ages of plainsong and Gregorian chant but re-emerged with the Renaissance. All the same, her heyday was really the 19th century. She appealed to the Pre-Raphaelites as well as Big-D Decadents like Baudelaire and small-d decadents like Swinburne.

Among the most extraordinary of her followers were Michael Field – 'were' in the plural because he was in fact two poets, aunt and niece, who were also lovers. Aunt Katherine Bradley was fourteen years older than her niece, Edith Cooper. The aunt died aged sixty-six in 1914, a year after Edith. For a time, they were on the edge of the Aesthetic Movement. They knew Wilde and Pater. They also knew Browning, who may have outed them. Book sales fell off after

93

that, possibly because people were shocked but also possibly because they were pretty poor poets. "Books I have of long ago,/And today; I shall not know/Some, unless thou read them, so/Their excelling /Music needs thy voice's flow." Or, worse: "Come with thy sun-governed mouth,/Thou wilt never suffer drouth." They had a private income from a Birmingham tobacco factory owned by their father/maternal grandfather. Richmond-on-Thames, a far cry from the temples and hills of Mytilene, was where they eventually settled. They converted later in life to Roman Catholicism, leaving the pagan Sappho behind.

Sappho's *Poem 58* is about being old. It too has had a strange history. Ten lines have been known – I think I'm right in saying – since Grenfell (the Egyptologist) and Hunt (the papyrologist) found them in that rubbish dump outside Oxyrhynchus in Egypt sometime between 1898 and 1908. The papyrus they uncovered dates from the 2nd century AD. Some scholars later tacked a four line ending to this ten line poem. Others, as is the way of scholars, said they didn't fit. Things stood like that until 2002 when some new lines by Sappho came on the market and were bought by Cologne University. These new poems were probably copied in the 3rd century BC, possibly for an anthology. The papyrus they were written on had been used as a mummy's wrappings. Among the strips was the opening couplet of *Poem 58* and it was published for the first time in 2004. Here is the complete poem, along with the disputed ending. The first sixteen lines are from Marguerite Johnson's book *Sappho*. The final couplet is from an essay by Deborah Boedeker in *The New Sappho on Old Age*.

> *Be passionate for the beautiful gifts of the fragrant-breasted*
> *Muses, O children, and for the clear, sweet-singing lyre.*
> *Old age has now seized my once-tender body; my hair has*
> *become light instead of dark.*
> *My heart has grown heavy; my knees refuse to support me,*
> *which once upon a time were as lithe for the dance as fawns.*

> *They say that rosy-armed Dawn, mad with love, once*
> *carried Tithonus to the end of the world;*
> *Beautiful and youthful then, but in time grey age engulfed*
> *him, he the husband of a goddess.*
> *But I cherish refinement and, thanks to Eros, I have*
> *obtained the brilliance and beauty of the Sun.*

Ellen Greene, also in an essay in *The New Sappho on Old Age*, gives a slightly different translation of that last couplet:

> *I love delicacy ... Eros has granted me the beauty and the*
> *brightness of the sun.*

(Eos, the Dawn, of course, fell for Tithonus when he was a young and handsome man. She asked Zeus to grant him eternal life but forgot to add 'and eternal youth'. He grew old, and older, from wizened doddering to total squeaking decrepitude, unable to die. Eos locked him in a room, where presumably he's still squeaking away today.)

Sappho may or may not have included that final stanza in her original verse but it does give *Poem 58* a stronger ending, making it into a kind of sonnet – setting out a problem or idea, developing it, solving or resolving it in the last few lines. Milton, for example, begins his sonnet *On His Blindness* by saying his talents are useless because he can't see. God will chide him for doing nothing. Then the idea is developed: what can God expect of a blind man? Patience replies: 'God asks only that you bear his yoke. Others will rush about serving Him'. Then there's the resolution: "They also serve who only stand and wait."

You can read *Poem 58* in the same way. It begins with a plea to children to study the arts – they expand consciousness, the purpose of human life – because every child will in time grow old. The poet already is, her life is nearly done and there's no help for it: even Tithonus, who married a goddess, was helpless before the crush, the onrush, of time. But there's 95 more to life than that – eternity is visible through the beauty of the sun, a gift of the power of love.

CHAPTER TEN

Reason Rising

By the end of the 5th century, the Roman Empire in the West was finished, taken over by barbarians from the north and east: Visigoths, Goths, Vandals, Ostrogoths – something which gave 'vandalism' a bad name and the Renaissance a name for Medieval cathedrals. The Empire lived on in the Greek east where Constantine rebuilt old Byzantium as Constantinople in the early 4th century, but the West was effectively isolated in the Dark Ages, a name coined by Petrarch.

There have been three renaissances: the Carolingian in the 8th century when Latin and literacy began to be taught in Cathedral schools. The one we just call The Renaissance. But there was also a mini-Renaissance in the 12th century by which time the Dark Ages were over. Some people object to the phrase, Dark Ages, because they weren't all that dark but they *were* different from what followed. What made them dark? Without pushing the idea too far, I'd suggest, that the loss of the Aristotelian strand of consciousness was a factor because it un-balanced the Western mind.

Some of Aristotle's logic had been known since the 6th century when Boethius translated it into Latin. Plato's Dialogues were unknown but a kind of Platonism had been there all along: just as Marxists don't have to read Marx, so Platonists don't have to read Plato. Platonism was known partly through St Augustine, partly through a partial translation of the *Timaeus,* but also through the Christianised Neo-Platonism of the Pseudo-Dionysius who lived in the later 4th/early 5th century but was mistaken for the man whom St Paul had converted in Athens. He was also confused with St Denis, patron saint of France. Erigena had translated him into Latin in the 9th century. (Erigena was Irish: the Teutonic barbarians never reached Ireland, on the edge of a wild ocean, and some knowledge of Greek was kept alive in the monasteries there.)

The Greek past, which was to be the West's future, began to be recovered in the 11th and 12th centuries. With the fall of Toledo in 1085, to take just one example, Ptolemy's *Mathematical System* became available again. Thirty years later the Englishman, Adelard of Bath, went to Syria to translate Euclid (2nd century AD) into Latin. Around this time, too, more Aristotle was recovered bit by bit from Italian monastery libraries and in Sicily, a Greek island until the 9th century, which suggests that a lot of the old learning had been there all along and what was missing was a realisation of its worth or perhaps just a lack of people able to read it. In the end, the bulk of Aristotle had been recovered by the late 12th/early 13th centuries.

The Middle Ages gave us windmills, eye-glasses, horses' halters, whippletrees, blast furnaces, magnetic compasses, clockwork clocks. Stirrups dated from even earlier. Farming changed as well, partly through new inventions such as better ploughs with mouldboards and coulters for turning and deepening the furrow, and horse collars which let ploughmen harness horses rather than oxen. Another big change was the three-field system: one fallow, one under grain, one planted with beans which make their own nitrate fertiliser – all helped of course by the Medieval Warm Period. (The population of Britain, for example, probably went from half a million to five million, until the 14th century Black Death cut it back again.) The names of the inventors are unknown though the clock-maker may have been English and the first lens grinder was certainly Italian (it's no accident that Galileo had access to telescopes in the 16th/17th centuries).

Those two strands of consciousness also surfaced as Nominalism and Realism. Realists followed Plato, believing the Forms were real, although now re-branded Universals. Nominalists – from the Latin for 'name' – thought that's all they were, names. The 11th century was also the time when logic came back to the West. Lanfranc (1005-1089) was an Italian who became Archbishop of Canterbury in 1070. He used logic to prove that the bread and wine of the eucharist *did* change into the body and blood of Christ: if the underlying Aristotelian Form shapes 'substance', and if that underlying Form is Christ, then the matter so shaped will, while outwardly remaining wine and wafer, internally be divine.

St Anselm (1033-1109), a fellow Italian, followed Lanfranc as Primate of All England. As a young man, he'd walked over the Alps looking for an education but found it out of reach because of the cost. Instead he became a teaching assistant to Lanfranc who, at the time, taught novices at the Abbey of Bec in Normandy. As Archbishop, Anselm also used logic – in his case in the ontological argument to reassure believers that God existed: God is the greatest thing we can imagine: what exists is greater than what doesn't: therefore to be the greatest thing, God must exist. Aquinas pointed out one flaw in this: Anselm had confused 'essence' with 'existence': you can describe the essence of the Hydra but it still doesn't exist (not in material reality although it does in consciousness otherwise we couldn't talk about it).

Another proof was from the German monk Hugh of St Victor (c1096-1141). Self-consciousness argues for a soul: the soul knows it hasn't always been here: something must have made it: that something must be God. Interestingly, Hugh used reason in spite of being a mystic who, as he'd have seen it, had direct access to the divine. Both strands were in some kind of balance in his mind. This, I think, is the best of the proofs: as we have seen, science can't handle consciousness and, as we will see, Hugh could be on to something.

Robert Grosseteste (1175-1253) ended up as Bishop of Lincoln though born into a poor family in Suffolk. Plato had been a mathematician and thought maths was a useful introduction to eternity while Aristotle, who you could call a scientist, had no time for numbers. Bishop Grosseteste, all those centuries later, seems to have realised that you can't do much science without maths. In that respect he must be regarded as one of the distant progenitors of the Scientific Revolution: the Western mind was turning that way. He wrote about the 'metaphysics of light' (metaphysical because it shines directly from God) but also had something to say about the importance of testing ideas – to verify their truth and not, as we post-Popperians would say, to prove them wrong. He also picked out the importance of inductive reasoning, of closely watching particular things until they suggest a general law. The old Bishop also had thoughts, or at least made comments about, optics and microscopes and telescopes.

It's hard these days to keep up with the scholarly unpicking of ancient reputations: Roger Bacon (1214-1294) has been revised downwards since the beginning of the last century. All the same he did write about optics, refraction, reflection and magnifying lenses, the anatomy of the eye and brain, as well as finding fault with the Julian calendar. To Bacon, too, light was God shining, an emanation. He also envisaged – without Leonardo's sketches – aeroplanes and submarines. More interestingly, Bacon wrote under the protection of Pope Clement IV and there is some evidence of a feeling that, if it developed its science, Christendom/the West could lead the world. (His name-sake, Francis Bacon (1561-1626) *began* to formulate the scientific method around three hundred years later – hypothesis followed by experiment. In fact, he's said to have died of pneumonia contracted while stuffing a chicken with snow to see if refrigeration works.)

Peter Abelard (1079-11420) is best known today for a sex scandal, although some say he was the first really great logician since Antiquity. He reads like an alpha male, a Breton, born into the lesser nobility, who gave up his hereditary knighthood and estates near Nantes to follow the life of a philosopher which, in the 12th century, meant earning your keep by pulling in paying students or starving. He was so quick witted and fluent he couldn't be beaten in debate. But his private life was so lurid that, if lived today, it would dominate the press and TV channels for days on end.

The affair of Abelard and Héloïse is on the same level, some think, as Tristan and Isolde or Romeo and Juliet. Abelard was about forty, Héloïse perhaps twenty. He lodged in the house of her Uncle Fulbert, a canon of Notre Dame. They became lovers, she had a child (a boy called Astrolabe), they married in secret, the story broke and her brothers, egged on by the canon, castrated Abelard in his bed at dead of night. (She became a nun, he a monk but a rumbustious and uncontrollable one – he was once nearly murdered in a monastery in Brittany: he was in his fifties at the time and no wild youth.) One story maintains that, immediately on being mutilated, he alerted the Watch and had his brothers-in-law caught, castrated and blinded on the spot. True or not, it seems to give some idea of the man's character, or mettle.

Abelard was a Nominalist which automatically tells us a lot about his cast of mind – that he belonged to the non-spiritual strand of consciousness, albeit in the middle. But although Aristotelian consciousness was back, the Platonist one was still strong. We can see this in the dispute between Abelard and St Bernard of Clairvaux in 1140. The argument revolved around the nature and make-up of the Trinity. St Bernard said it couldn't be talked about: faith was all you needed. No, said Abelard, nothing is out of bounds to reason. There was to be a debate but in the end St Bernard dodged it by accusing Abelard of heresy. Abelard by-passed the Council which was set up to try him and set off for Rome to appeal to the Pope. Bernard, not yet a saint (needless to say), out-foxed him by writing to the Vatican, the postal service seemingly being quicker than walking or riding. The upshot was that the Pope ordered Abelard not only to keep quiet but to retire to a monastery. He ended his days peacefully in the Abbey at Cluny.

We know a lot about Abelard because he wrote an autobiography, *The Story of My Calamities,* which has survived along with letters to his wife. Among his other works is *Sic et Non – Yea and Nay* or *Yes and No.* It puts contradictory arguments, from Scripture and the Ancients, side by side in pairs. To get to the truth you need sceptical questioning, Abelard argued, which sounds a bit like the Socratic Method. In another book, *Scito Teipsum* (Know Thyself) he argued that sin is not in what you do but in being contemptuous of God while you're doing it, a suspiciously convenient belief for him, you might think. It may have been his opinion that the Crucifixion was a demonstration of God's love.

John Duns Scotus (1266-1308) was a Realist and probably, but not certainly, Scottish, from Duns in Berwickshire, if the clue really is in the name. To fellow scholastics he was known as the Subtle Doctor: from Duns we get 'dunce' because it describes most of us when it comes to understanding his subtlety. That subtlety lay in a mix of Aristotelian empiricism and the Platonist idea that you can know more than your senses tell you. Some of his ideas were not so subtle, though. Against Aquinas he argued that the Virgin Mary was sinless. He disagreed with St Augustine that we learn things when God illuminates the mind. (It's the other way around, as Cardinal Newman recognised: learning expands consciousness: an expanded consciousness illuminates the world for you.) Against Aquinas, Scotus argued for the primacy of God's Will over God's intellect: God wills your salvation before He works out why you deserve it: No, said Aquinas, He weighs up the why before the willing.

He's of interest to some of us now because of his influence on the 19th century Jesuit poet, Gerard Manley Hopkins, a man with mystical leanings (a Secret Friend, perhaps) who sensed the invisible through particular visible things – a flower, a water well, stooks of corn. In fact, he was so taken up with the particularity of things that he coined two words – inscape and instress – to single out and isolate its importance. At the same time, he worried that his private insight was unorthodox. Then, while studying in Stonyhurst, he came across the Scotist concept of 'haecceity' or 'thisness' and – mistakenly – associated it with his own thoughts on inscape, or the self-hood of individual things.

What exactly Scotus meant I'm not sure but we can read it like this: think of Aristotle's First Matter as primary potentiality waiting to actualise an unlimited number of secondary potentialities which, when realised, become every individual thing from a cup to the cosmos. The primary potentiality is 'whatness' or 'quiddity' while each of those actualised secondary potentialities has its own 'thisness' or 'haecceity'.

But did Scotus think that this thisness could lead back to whatness as I assume Hopkins did? Platonically speaking (but not Aristotelianly), whatness has to be part of the eternal realm and thisness must be connected to it. If so, anybody seeing thisness could be put in direct contact with eternity, thus triggering a mystical moment of higher or lower intensity. I'm not sure that Hopkins took it that far but, whatever the truth, he certainly felt a Doctor of the Church had given him permission to believe in his own private insight. Instress, his other coinage, seems to have been the force holding a thing together and so perhaps was also whatness (because without it there can be no thisness (inscape)).

Hopkins, grateful to the man who set his mind at rest, called him 'Of realty the rarest-veined unraveller' and wrote a poem about the Oxford where both he and Scotus had been students, although separated by centuries. The poem begins:

> Towery city and branchy between towers;
> Cuckoo-echoing, bell-swarmed, lark-charmed,
>   rook-racked, river-rounded;
> The dapple-eared lily below thee.

The words alone let you see the invisible beyond the visible whereas the analysing of its thisness and whatness would get in the way and blight it. And so we have another warning for the West, too much analysis can destroys that spiritual strand unless kept apart.

G K Chesterton wrote his short book, *St Thomas Aquinas,*

in 1933 and from a very Roman Catholic point of view (he was a convert). If he was right, the 13th century was not unlike the early 21st – a time of upheaval, change, excess, decay (as some saw it), with Europe threatened by enemies both within and without, two of which – Islam and Manichaeism (the Albigenses) – had no Greek background at all and so were completely alien. Adding to the sense of dissolution was the return of Aristotle, threatening the now stale Platonism of St Augustine, and a new breed of beggar-friars, the Franciscans and Dominicans, who were let out of the monasteries like "sparks from a furnace; the furnace of the abnormal love of God". Aquinas was a friar.

He was born near Naples, a younger son of Count Aquino, and very well connected – the Holy Roman Emperor was a second cousin, Barbarossa a great-uncle. The Dominicans, then newly formed, were sworn to poverty, study and preaching and were therefore quite unsuitable for a young nobleman. So his family kidnapped him and locked him in a tower of one of their castles until he changed his mind. He was an overweight ox-like man (so described by fellow students) with green eyes and, of course, the black and white garb of the Dominicans. He was so placid it's said he got angry only twice in his life of forty-nine years (1225-1274). The first was when, imprisoned in the tower, his family sent a heavily tarted-up young woman to tempt him to break his vow of chastity. He picked up a burning log from the fire, drove her from his room, then scorched a cross on the back of the door.

In the end, of course, he got his way and went to study under St Albertus Magnus, a German Dominican, in Cologne and then in Paris. Albert was eclectic when it came to ideas, taking them from Augustine and Neo-Platonism as well as Aristotle. He also took an interest in botany and zoology, doing some research of his own, believing that observations had to be empirical and results verifiable. He introduced Aquinas to Aristotle, the younger man's life work: the old joke, in fact, was that Aristotle Aristotelianised

Aquinas and Aquinas Christianised Aristotle.

What was the Aquinan achievement? In Chesterton's opinion he saved us from Augustinian Platonism by 'bringing God back to earth' by raising reasoning to its highest level: reasoning about the physical world *has* to lead to God because God made them both: faith will come, through grace, if you reason well and hard enough. In other words, he re-set the twin strands of consciousness to run, not in parallel, but towards a single point, God. His second bout of anger, in fact, was against Siger of Brabant who tried to make out that he believed in two disconnected truths, two distinct and unmeeting strands of thought.

Aquinas also took over Aristotle's ideas of eudemony and teleology. Happiness – or excellence or fulfilled potential – is the proper end of us all. To get there we have to obey the Moral Law which is expressed on earth as Natural Law to which man-made laws have to conform. Politically, he also sided with Aristotle: a State's only job is to clear a space in which people can perfect themselves. He also clarified the concept of the Just War (first proposed by St Augustine): a war fought for a good cause, ordered by legitimate authority, with peace as its aim.

Aquinas was also a bit of an anti-capitalist before there was a capitalism to be against. Things which people made for themselves, he said, were always better than those they made for trade. Worse: "trade, insofar as it aims at making profits, is most reprehensible, since the desire for gain knows no bounds but reaches into the infinite." Chesterton agreed, but then he was a Distributist and so was anti-capitalist (and anti-socialist) himself. You have, in fact, to be wary of Chesterton's unblinking faith in all things Catholic. Some friars, he really did believe, had seen Aquinas floating in the air after a carving of Christ had climbed down from the Cross to tell him that what he'd written about the eucharist was quite right.

Aquinas is best known today for his five proofs of God's existence. All five are found in his *Summa Theologica*:

Things change when a potential inside them is actualised

by something which is already partly actualised. What is only potential can't actualise anything so there must be a fully actualised Something to set the chain of changes going.

Change is caused but causes can't stretch away endlessly at both ends. Change therefore has to have a fixed, unchanging starting point.

If a thing doesn't have to exist, then once upon a time it didn't. If everything doesn't have to exist, then once nothing did. But if at one time there were nothing, nothing could exist now because nothing can come out of nothing. Therefore something has always existed.

Some things are better than others so there must be an ultimate Best.

Everything has a wired-in end-point to which it's drawn. All things follow their built-in guidelines even though most things aren't conscious. Some supreme intelligence, therefore, wrote the rules.

Usually it's said that none of these proofs prove God's existence. That may be true but some of them do seem to prove that Plato was right about the Forms. Cosmologists say something can come out of nothing and physicists say particles are appearing out of nowhere all the time. But to some people the existence of those free-standing abstractions (Beauty, Being) seems self-evident – though not to Aquinas who thought you can't take the maths out of matter: no matter, no maths – and they are clearly more like Plato's Ideas than they are like God. In some other ways, too, Aquinas seemed to have flirted with Plato. Things exist, for example, because God actualises ideas held in His own mind, as an architect makes a house out of an immaterial concept in his head. There's also something Platonic about the two strands of consciousness converging: you could say that consciousness is a spectrum running from Being to Becoming and back.

In fact, Aquinas is said to have stopped writing when he had what could have been a mystical experience: Plato trumped Aristotle and he had no more to say. He was canonised without a miracle to his name because his ideas were miracles in themselves.

As we've seen, we can follow the two strands of consciousness through about three hundred years of the Middle Ages. In the 12th century theology and philosophy were, if not fused, at least confused with one another. The 13th separated and tried to synthesise them. By the 14th the two were following separate tracks, a change which was noted at the time: the *via antiqua* was the old way, *via moderna* the new – the Occamist – way based partly on fresh ideas about logic. Nominalism was now sometimes called *terminism* because the universals were nothing but 'terms' and Occam's philosophy became more like the analytical kind of the 20th century's Anglosphere. A lot of time was spent analysing propositions.

William of Occam (1287-1347) was sixty-two years younger than Aquinas and a real 14th century man. He was born in a village called Ockham – there's one in Surrey, another in Yorkshire – and his empiricism is typically English: for centuries, it was the core philosophy of England, one reason – perhaps the main one – why union with a rationalist Europe has never been easy. With the West's decline, the power of empiricism may also be waning, replaced by nothing in particular.

Today he's most famous for Occam's Razor (a phrase he never used) – a simple, elegant solution is more likely to be right than a clumsy, complicated one. He was also against all attempts at proving God's existence because logic denies it can be done. Names were all the old philosophers were talking about, not reality. You can't prove you have a soul or that it's immortal any more than you can prove people have free will. Why? Because proof would need 'necessary deductions from necessary principles', as Father Copleston put it in *Medieval Philosophy*. God and the soul are knowable only through faith and that's the end of it. He was also against too much Papal power, favouring a council to temper it. In 1323 he sided with Ludwig of Bavaria after he'd been elected

Holy Roman Emperor and after Pope John XXII said he'd need Papal approval before being confirmed. Occam also believed the people had the right to turn a king off his throne if he acted against them. There was no such thing as divine right or Papal supremacy.

The 14th century also threw up a few startling spikes of modernity – using maths to solve new problems, for example. The men behind it had all been students at Merton College, Oxford, and so are known collectively as the Merton or Oxford Calculators. The three best known are Thomas Bradwardine (c.1290-1349), Richard Swineshead (no accurate dates but he was active between 1340 and 1355) and William Heytesbury who lived between 1313 and 1373. Their stories are told in James Hannam's *God's Philosophers*.

Bradwardine briefly ended up as Archbishop of Canterbury until he died of the plague or Black Death. He worked out a mathematical formula to explain Aristotle's theory of motion (things move because they're pushed and keep on moving because they keep on being pushed) and was wrong only because so was Aristotle. Swineshead worked out the speed of a weight falling down a hole drilled to the centre of the earth although he, too, got the answer wrong. Heytesbury looked for the answer to the problem: "what happens when a moving object accelerates at a constant rate?" His answer (in Hannam's words) is still called "the mean speed theorem by historians, and is central to physics because it describes the motion of an object, any object, under gravity." (Books by both Swineshead and Heytesbury were among the first to be printed on the new moveable type presses in the next century, the 15th.)

Paris took matters farther. Nicholas of Oresme (1320/25-1382), for example, worked out that a car (to modernise a little) uniformly accelerating from 0-10 mph will cover the same distance in the same time as one travelling steadily at 5 mph. To make ideas like these more understandable, he invented the graph. He also argued that the earth *could* orbit the sun without the air streaming away into space, though he didn't believe it himself. John Buridan (1300-1358) – following on from John Philoponus in the 6th century AD – argued for impetus: a thrown pebble will sail on forever unless other things stop it: on earth those things are mainly air and gravity.

Alongside all of this, there ran a very deep Platonist strand which surfaced as mysticism: Hugh and Richard of St Victor (12th century): the author of *Ancren Riwle* (Rules for Anchoresses), Thomas de Hales, St Bonavetura (13th): Richard Rolle, Walter Hylton, Julian of Norwich, the author of *The Cloud of Unknowing*, Eckhart, Ruysbroeck, Suso, Tauler (14th). Eckhart was the greatest of them and he too had trouble with the creator concept. To him, the Trinity and each human soul were one and the same, each an upthrust of a universal Godhead like a mountain with foothills and knolls rising from a common earth. That was heresy, of course, and he was condemned for it.

An interesting annexe to 14th century history illustrates the two kinds of consciousness perfectly. Mysticism seemed to be in the European air at that time, in the Catholic West and the Orthodox East. In the Greek Church it took the form of the mystical methodology of Hesychasm (meaning 'peace, silence, stillness'). It blossomed mainly among the monks of Mount Athos but, of course, had its roots in Platonism – via Clement of Alexandria (2nd century), Plotinus (3rd), St Athanasius and two of the three Cappadocian Fathers (Basil and Gregory of Nyssa) in the 4th, Psuedo-Dionysius the Areopogite (the St Denis of Suger) in the 5th/6th. It *may* have been elaborated in the 10th/11th by Symeon the New Theologian (949-1022). If he were the man behind it, he worked out a simple, Zen-like method for inducing mystical experiences – sit quietly, chin on chest, look inward, control breath, intone (mantra-like) the Jesus Prayer: "Lord Jesus Christ, Son of God, have mercy on me, a sinner."

What was experienced was the 'uncreated light of God', which is a problem in Christianity because God is unseeable. It was also described as the same celestial light witnessed by the Apostles on Mount Tabor during the Transfiguration of Christ. In the 14th century things came to a head with two factions facing each other. On the Hesychast side stood St Gregory Palamas (1296-1359) representing the Platonist wing of consciousness. Palamas began as a monk on Athos and ended as Archbishop of Thessalonica. Against him, on the side of Aristotelian consciousness, stood Barlaam (1290-1348). He was an Italian from Calabria, a Greek-speaker of Greek extraction. He died, probably of the Black Death, as Bishop of Gerace in Calabria, either having converted or reverted to Catholicism. Given his background, it's not unlikely (though it is disputed) that he was latinising Nominalist supporter of Aquinan Scholasticism. (Barlaam, I believe, taught Petrarch Greek.) He took against hesychasm, calling it heretical, blasphemous and ditheistic. The dispute between the two sides led to a series of Councils in Constantinople until Hesychasm was finally accepted. What hesyschasts experienced, it was decided, was the 'energy', not the 'essence', of God – an idea dating back to the 4th century Cappadocian Fathers.

Scholasticism was all about reason and as such tended to downplay grace while emphasising justification through merit – you get what you deserve. In time Luther rejected that. Once you start to apply logical to the a-logical, things will begin to break unless you keep a well developed Platonist-type consciousness in being as well. Greek Orthodoxy stuck to tradition, putting more faith in Faith than in reason. In consequence it kept going in spite of Islamic invasions and Communist persecutions but it had no Scientific Revolution or Enlightenment and yet may well still be around if the Western end of the West disintegrates.

Looking back, then, we can see the 11th century butterfly already flapping its wings and so causing the anti-spiritual gales we're living through in the 21st. At the same time, we can also still see some of the physical good things which came of that reunion, and will do so in the next chapter.

CHAPTER ELEVEN

The Gothic IS Platonic

In *Civilisation*, his 1960s TV series, Kenneth Clark seemed to feel uneasily that all was not right in the West, but not once did he suggest that de-spiritualisation, or the loss of a Platonic outlook, a shrinking of consciousness, was part of the problem. On the other hand, he was aware of the spiritual, something rare even then. He reported, for example, that Georges Clemenceau had urged Monet, when he was an old man, half-blinded by cataracts, to keep on painting, to immerse himself, as Clark put it, in "a pool of memories and sensations." "Total immersion," he went on, "is a means by which we can lose our identity in the whole and gain thereby a more intense consciousness of being". At the beginning of the series he spoke about sensing the presence of "some God" in Iona where the light filled him with a sense of peace and freedom.

He was also at his best when talking about the spirituality of the 12th century renaissance and its greatest spiritual achievement – Gothic cathedrals. In 1135, Abbot Suger was in charge of the Abbey of St Denis in Cluny, now a suburb of Paris. He was a tiny man who believed the English were destined forever to be subordinate to the French. Suger, it seems, had read the Pseudo-Dionysius thinking it had been written by St Denis, patron saint of his own Abbey as well as of France. That the saint hadn't doesn't matter. What does is what Suger got out of it – pure Platonism: Beauty is God therefore you can reach Him through beautiful things. "Man may rise to the contemplation of the divine through the senses," said the Abbot. "The dull mind rises to truth through that which is material." The outcome was Gothic architecture, built around pointed arches, flying buttresses and rib vaults. "Bright is the noble edifice," said the Abbot, "that is pervaded by new light." So masons installed stained glass windows to colour the new, floating, airy spaces. (Abelard, incidentally, had been sent to St Denis after his troubles with Héloïse and her family. He was expelled for mocking the monks for being something less than holy.)

Clark went on to say that Chartres, finished in 1164, is also a legacy of this Medieval Platonism. The shape of the cathedral, on its hill overlooking the River Eure and the plain of Beauce, is based on the Pythagorean vision of numbers, a mathematics of harmony, which rule the cosmos and keep it in being. Parts of the West in the 12th century, Clark told his viewers, were shot through with spirituality: whole villages turned out to help the masons who were building Chartres. They hauled cart loads of stone in total silence, bringing gifts of wine, bread and oil. Inside, he went on, is one of the two greatest covered spaces in the world – the other being in the former Christian church of Hagia Sophia (Holy Wisdom) in what is now Istanbul.

The cult of Mary also took off in the 12th century (Chartres, its builders said, was where the Virgin felt most at home on earth) and St Bernard of Citaux told us why: like Aphrodite before her, Mary was the embodiment of that spiritual Beauty which links heaven and earth. (Does this explain the 'courtly love' of the troubadours? That odd idea of a man being so in thrall to a woman, who is physically and socially out of his reach, that he spends half a lifetime writing poetry to her?)

Statues of Greek philosophers are carved around the arch of one of the great doors at Chartres. The main facade of the Cathedral is, in fact, famous for its statues, the best of which are elongated figures of an unknown king and queen. Clark compared them to the Greek art of the 5th century BC in their stillness and restraint. They're Greek also in the "simplicity in every fold" of their gowns. So Greek-like, in fact, that the man who carved them must have seen Greek sculpture in the south of France. In particular, the faces are striking and were then new (unique (perhaps) in that they radiated spirituality. But, Clark went on to ask, what comes first – a good face or good sculpture? Look in tomorrow's newspapers, he told his viewers in 1969: good faces have all gone and so, therefore, has good sculpture.

Just over a hundred years later we had the 14th century line-up – Petrarch, Eckhart, Occam and Dante. Europe could have gone all of these way but two were dead-ends – Eckhart's mysticism and Dante's Aristotelian cosmology – while Petrarch led to the Renaissance and Occam to empiricism. Empiricism has been the winner. Instead of two streams – the spiritual and the secular, mind and matter – Occam has been elevated over the lot.

Petrarch, according to P O Kristeller, was a humanist – *umanista* being scholarly Renaissance slang for somebody devoted to the study and expansion of rhetoric, poetry, history, grammar and moral philosophy through the study of old texts, both those already known and those, once lost, then coming back to Western Europe from old Byzantium. Petrarch has to be distinguished from philosophers like Ficino and Pico della Mirandola. One, as Frances Yates put it, "sees man in relation to society: the other sees him in relation to the cosmos.' Petrarch was a Becoming man, Ficino aimed at joining Being – so, once again, we have two strands of consciousness.

One day in April 1336, Petrarch climbed Mont Ventoux, all six thousand feet of it, in Provence. From the summit you can see the Alps, the Rhône valley and the Bay of Marseilles. It gets windy up there (though the name doesn't seem to come from the French *le vent*) and his copy of St Augustine's *Confessions* blew open at the page with this passage: "And men go about to wonder at the heights of the mountains, and the mighty waves of the sea, and the wide sweep of rivers, and the circuit of the ocean, and the revolution of the stars, but themselves they consider not."

"I closed the book," Petrarch wrote, "angry with myself that I should still be admiring earthly things who might long ago have learned from even the pagan philosophers that nothing is wonderful but the soul, which, when great itself, finds nothing great outside itself." He added: "We look about us for what is to be found only within." In that, he was a pure *umanista*. He'd stood on the summit of a mountain surrounded by the second hand things which lead to the first hand and rejected them out of hand. Plato said that what you see is a poor decaying material copy of what's eternal, pure and perfect. Eyes can't see it, mind can, but not Petrarch's. He was thirty-two, exactly at the mid-point of life like Dante in the dark wood.

They say Petrarch was a forerunner of the Renaissance because he saw that Europe had lost its way and needed to go back to its beginnings to start again. The classics, Petrarch argued, were as spiritual and moral as Christianity and they had deeper insights into what it is to be human. Their emphasis was on people. The Greeks had other things to offer as well: if you get clarity into your writing, you clarify your soul: outward grace of style promotes inward grace. Human greatness was the Greek ideal and you reached it through culture and free-thinking creativity.

The Renaissance proper had to wait another hundred or so years. Frances Yates, writing in the early years of the Second World War, pointed out that the pre-Aquinan Middle Ages were more Platonist than Aristotelian. That Platonist strain was always there, so that the Renaissance – rather than starting all over again – just brought previously unknown individual books from the Byzantine East to Florence in the 15th century. Pletho, one of the Greek scholars who brought them, believed in Apollo and Aphrodite, rightly too it you look at them as forces of the nature which have to be obeyed. Rightly also the new Platonism filled the world with a new enchantment: Aphrodite and Apollo were beauty and love, intellect and light.

In the second half of the 15th century, Ficino set up a kind of floating Platonist Academy in Florence, which was then ruled by Cosimo de Medici. Ficino developed a religious philosophy based on Neo-Platonism. (Ficino and Pico, it should be said, were deceived by Hermeticism, thinking it was real Platonism.) From genuine Neo-Platonism came the idea that the world is made of the overflow of the Good and so divinity infuses nature. But if divinity is everywhere, then all places are holy, not just the space inside churches. Against the Church's collectivised ritual was set Platonism's inner spirituality.

Renaissance Platonism was also the real beginning of the Scientific Revolution which did so much to undo Christianity. It began, not with Aristotle's life sciences, but with maths-based astronomy. The church, ironically, needed an accurate calendar and the calendar was inaccurate because Ptolemaic geo-centric astronomy was wrong. Copernicus (the solar system is heliocentric) and Kepler (the planets move in ellipses) shared Plato's belief that the super-lunar heavens must be ruled by precise but simple mathematical rules – after all, Pythagoras had taught that numbers themselves are both numinous and sacred. Ficino's sacralisation of the sun must have helped as well – it was so sacred, he argued, that it couldn't possibly move around the lowly earth.

Study astronomy, Plato said. The Heavens were created out of Chaos by the Demiurge and move in accordance with the mathematical Idea, so they are Divine Reason displayed as matter and are therefore spiritually perfect and therefore make the divine directly accessible. The only snag was the wandering planets – a hitch solved by Kepler's ellipses: the regularity, as I understand it, comes not from the perfect circularity of their orbits but from the areas they sweep out.

The Renaissance, moving only slowly north, got to Shakespeare's England by the end of the 16th century. Frances Yates also pointed out that Giordano Bruno's *De Gli Eroici Furori* (*The Heroic Frenzies*), a book about love as the way to Being, was dedicated to Sir Philip Sydney. "The possibility therefore suggests itself," she wrote, "that if

Elizabethan philosophical poetry may be the heir to a Platonic tradition which had left the universities, then Elizabethan love poetry may be the spiritual heir of the ruined abbeys and monasteries" which had been Platonist long before Aristotle became fashionable. The old 'holy philosophy', therefore, may still have been a living thing in late Renaissance England.

Some of Shakespeare's opinions, she further suggested, were distantly Platonic – not at second hand, but at many hands distance. For example, his belief in the harmony of the universe and how people are governed by it. Berowne's speech in *Love's Labour's Lost,* praising love as the greatest teacher, might have come indirectly from *The Symposium* via Ficino's commentaries. The Academy in the play could have been a copy of Ficino's Academy which was a copy of Plato's (which brings to mind Plato's strictures on art as a copy of a copy of the real thing).

We're familiar with the idea that the plots and characters of several of Shakespeare's plays were taken from Sir Thomas North's translation of Plutarch (46-120 AD) – *Antony and Cleopatra, Julius Caesar, Coriolanus, Timon of Athens.* The burnished throne speech in *Antony and Cleopatra* is almost a straight lift – it *is* plagiarised – from Plutarch:

> *The barge she sat in, like a burnished throne,*
> *Burned on the water: the poop was beaten gold;*
> *Purple the sails, and so perfumèd, that*
> *The winds were lovesick with them; the oars were silver,*
> *Which to the tune of flutes kept stroke, and made*
> *The water which they beat to follow faster,*
> *As amorous of their strokes.*

Less well known is the fact that Plutarch was a pious follower of Middle Platonism – a philosophy seeking a concrete way to God. It was intellectual and had invented a strange array of gods and daemons to help believers climb through the hierarchy. Middle Platonism was neither mystical nor Platonist in the spiritual sense. But then neither was Shakespeare.

Why didn't the Renaissance add more to Western thought? Clark asked. Because, he replied, those thoughts were expressed in stone and paint, not in printer's ink. However, he missed out something that was also important. In the index to his book of the series, Neoplatonism is listed once only. Yet surely what made the Renaissance was the recovery of the spiritual insights of Plato and Plotinus? At the mystical level, both are deeper than Christianity and could therefore add to it. Each person has a bit of divinity lodged inside them and so can be spiritually illuminated. Three hundred years after Abbot Suger, the Olympian gods also made a come back – Aphrodite is Love and Beauty, not only a force of nature but a pure Platonic Form as well. Apollo is light and intellect. These forces of nature lead directly to Plato's upper sphere of unchanging perfection. They mean, too, that this sublunar world is suffused with divinity.

In other words, the Renaissance did add something to Western thought, it's just that the West has forgotten it. Power shifted to northern Europe and to Reformed – that is, de-Hellenised – Christianity, Bible-based and starkly bleak. By the late 17th century the Industrial Revolution had already begun in England with a banking system, the Bank of England, stable politics, the rule of law (including contract law) and early steam engines pumping water out of Cornish tin and copper mines. The Industrial Revolution also needed Locke's empiricism and Newton's Laws – a clock-work cosmos run by rules which can be learned and turned against matter to force it to behave the way you want. Feelings of emptiness were inevitable and, to fill the void, utopias were invented to take the place of a failed supernatural religion. As consciousness shrank, even the unspiritual had to find alternatives: materialists found one in Marx. Others, however, could still break free on their own and, as an unlikely example, we can look at Oscar Wilde, however counter-intuitive that might seem.

CHAPTER TWELVE

Applied Platonism

W hat was the Aesthetic Movement all about? Why did it fail, after forty years, around 1900? The satirists may not have known why but they did know pretension when they saw it. In *Patience,* Gilbert wrote:

> *Though the Philistines may jostle,*
> *you will rank as an apostle*
> *in the high aesthetic band,*
> *If you walk down Piccadilly*
> *with a poppy or a lily*
> *in your medieval hand.*

George du Maurier drew a cartoon for *Punch.* An aesthetic bridegroom and his aesthetic bride gaze aesthetically at an aesthetic teapot. Groom: "It is quite consummate, is it not?" Bride: "Oh, Algernon, let us live up to it!"

Walter Pater, the brains behind it all, said in his novel, *Marius the Epicurean,* that people can "make themselves perfect by the worship of beauty". In his *Studies in the History of the Renaissance* he says people should look "not for the fruit of experience but experience itself. Success in life is to burn always with this hard gemlike flame."

Oscar Wilde, who really did walk down Piccadilly, not with a poppy but certainly with a lily, was less sure, at least to begin with. When his ship docked in New York on his first trip to the US, a journalist asked him for a definition of Aestheticism. Wilde was stumped. All he could say was: "a search for the beautiful." Later he added: "It is the science of the beautiful through which men seek the correlation of the arts" whatever that means. Also it is: ".. the search for the secret of life." Then, more interestingly he said: If you beautify the outer, you beautify the inner.

For some time in Oxford, it had been a case of Ruskin v Pater, the spiritual versus the secular. For Ruskin the aesthetic led to the spiritual, for Pater it was all a matter of the senses. (Pater did talk of going into 'ecstasies' but they might have been of the poppy-lily pretentious type, not the St Teresa kind.) On the whole (until he turned to socialism) Ruskin had an upper and lower world, Pater only a lower. At first Wilde sided with Pater. "Who, as Mr Pater suggests somewhere, would exchange the curve of a single rose-leaf for the formless intangible Being which Plato rates so high? What to us is the Illumination of Philo, the Abyss of Eckhart, the Vision of Boehme, the monstrous Heaven itself that was revealed to Swedenborg's blinded eyes? Such things are less than the yellow trumpet of one daffodil of the field, far less than the meanest of the visible arts."

But Aestheticism had a built-in problem which Kierkegaard picked on long before the Movement began: the aesthete couldn't savour the experience because he had to cling so tightly to it. Pater also failed to see that experiences can be good or bad, and the bad ones aren't good for you no matter how startling. Perhaps Wilde all along sensed that art for art's sake wasn't enough. The reason for thinking this is to be found in his novel, *The Picture of Dorian Gray,* which came out in 1890, when Wilde was thirty-six. Right from the beginning, the protagonist (he's hardly a hero) is looking for more than mere gem-like flames: he wants to "spiritualise the senses". Not that he ever does: the whole book is a catalogue of vice, depravity, deviance, debauchery – Gray is so debased that few of his escapades are described, his readership of course being a late Victorian one. 'Exquisite' is the most commonly used word about these experiences, followed by 'charm', 'charming', 'charmed' – all of them a misuse of words. The book revolves around Gray's portrait, the Picture of the title. The face in the painting becomes more and more ravaged, more brutal looking, cruel and depraved with every act of grossness by the living Gray who remains young, unblemished, handsome.

Things get worse when he comes into a legacy – a stately home and estate with all its income. Now a rich man, he's freer than ever to do what he wants – buy exquisiteness and lurid experience. The woman who loves him (he loves nobody) kills herself when he rejects her: she was an actress until love took away her need to act and so she was no longer 'exquisite', not to Gray any way. Then he murders the artist who painted his portrait and blackmails a friend into getting rid of the corpse. The friend then kills himself. The East End opium dens are filled with well-born young men whom Gray has ruined. Women he's seduced sell themselves in the lowest dives by the docks.

All the while, his portrait grows more and more raddled while he, after eighteen years of unbridled licentiousness, hasn't aged a day. In the end, however, he sees how wrong he's been and repents but only after he's nearly murdered by the brother of the long dead actress. Will repentance make the picture young again? Gray rushes to see. It hasn't changed and he slashes it with a knife. Next day the servants find him dead, stabbed through the heart, as ravaged as the picture had been – *had* been because it is now as unblemished as on that summer's day when the paint first dried.

In the novel, Gray is inspired by a book whose title is never given but which is generally thought to have been *A Rebours* by Huysmans. The title is often translated *Against Nature*.

The following year Wilde brought out a rather odd book – *The Soul of Man Under Socialism*. We have to remember that Lenin and the Revolution were still twenty-six years away in the future, because Wilde's vision of socialism is nothing like the reality it turned out to be in the 20th century, and how it is today.

To begin with, Wilde's socialism was not about the collective or the statist but about setting the individual free. Property ownership is a bore because it entails tiresome duties. Socialism would abolish property and, with it, poverty. Socialism is about being, not owning or having. Without property all can live, not just exist. You can create the perfect man if you have perfect conditions. Under socialism, true personality will flourish and grow naturally without argument or discord. People will know everything, own nothing: it will be beautiful, with no jealousy, no laws, no authority. There'll be no punishments at all because punishment increases crime: what little crime there might be will be treated by doctors as the mental illness it is. Criminals aren't criminals at all – they're people who are starving. It won't be a question of *know thyself* but *be thyself* – that was Christ's real message when he said the poor have developed personalities, the rich undeveloped ones. "Develop your perfection within. Riches are within. Material things not only don't matter, they get in the way of inner growth."

Socialism will also abolish marriage and the family which, again, was what Jesus wanted. You can't conform and be free. The state will exist but only as a 'voluntary association' of people who choose to get together to organise labour and make things for use. The state will make what is useful: individuals will make what is beautiful. All disgusting manual work will be done by machines – coal mining, stoking furnaces, running messages. Until now, machines have put men out of work to enrich a single owner: under Socialism all will benefit.

Half way through the book – it's very short – something must have upset him: he switches to a attack on the middle classes, and into a defence of art and in doing so unwittingly reveals what real socialism was going to be like when it did come along – controlling and contemptuous. "Art is the most intense mode of individualism that the world has known." He's inclined to say the '*only* intense mode'. If the artist doesn't create for his own pleasure, he's no artist. Because art is so intensely individualist, the public want to control it. They want art to be popular, and "to please their want of taste, to flatter their absurd vanity, to tell them what they have been told before." They want to be amused and distracted.

Art shouldn't try to be popular – instead ordinary people should try to be artists. Poetry has escaped public control because nobody reads it: the public insult poets but leave their work alone. Novels and plays, on the other hand, are different and if they're vulgar and silly it's because the public is. Wilde sees the artist almost as a revolutionary continually pushing at the boundaries. It's as though the artist can do no wrong, the public no right. No work of art can be morbid because morbidity can't be expressed (although *Dorian Gray* was a bit gruesome). The public are morbid because they can't express anything. Vulgar and stupid is that they are.

Journalists are like tradesmen providing customers with what they want, and the best of them are ashamed of themselves. They're wrong to report on the private lives of public men, who shouldn't be gossiped about. In France they do things better: there, divorce cases are merely noted, not reported in detail. Here journalists are too free, while artists are cramped. In France it's the other way around.

The sole problem is this – the public want to dictate to artists what art should be. Instead they should shut up and believe what they're told, take what's given to them and try to live up to it because the public is to be acted upon, not to act. The public should accept, not think. The true artist writes for himself, not the public.

Towards the end of the book, Wilde reverts to his socialist theme: under socialism there'll be no diseases, no dull work, only 'joy in the contemplation of the joyous life of others."

Even though Wilde – or anybody else at the time – couldn't know what socialism was going to be like, this is beyond all common sense. Not even the most unworldly could think it might be true yet his plays, it now appears, were written as revolutionary tracts to bring down the system, obliterate the middle classes and set up a socialist state in the ruins. How many people watching *The Importance of Being Earnest* realise they're being brainwashed?

Add to that his endless and not very funny epigrams – "I never travel without my diary. One should always have something sensational to read in the train" and, worse, his mock-deep ones: "We are all in the gutter, but some of us are looking at the stars" – and you have a portrait of rather intolerant, narrow-minded, self-obsessed, self-righteous, emotionally unstable, clever and mentally lightweight (physically overweight) middle class man who was a bit too immature for middle age.

Then, four years after *The Soul of Man*, all that changed when he was sent down for sodomy and imprisoned in Reading jail. He was a man least able to handle life in a late Victorian prison yet his best work – *The Ballad of Reading Jail* and *De Profundis* – came out of it. *De Profundis* – from the depths – *is* deep. The contrast with the old Wilde is extreme: who'd have thought he had such depth in him.

Richard Ellmann, his biographer, said *De Profundis* was a kind of dramatic monologue and a love letter to Bosie, Lord Alfred Douglas, the immediate cause of his downfall. It's much more than that. Half is about Bosie's wrong doing and an attempt to fix things between them. A lot, immodestly, is about his own genius – it's an "elegy for lost greatness," as he put it, calling himself the symbol of art and culture for his age. "The gods have given me almost everything. I had genius a distinguished name, high social position, brilliancy, intellectual daring." "I alter the lives of men and the colours of things: there was nothing I said that did not make people wonder."

But that is the shallow end of his spectrum and we should keep our minds on the deeper part. He learned humility in jail – defined as the "frank acceptance of all experience". But he also learned the importance, not of being earnest, but of suffering and sorrow. "Suffering is the means by which we exist, because it is the only means by which we become conscious of existing." We have to remember past suffering as evidence of a 'continued identity'.

"Where there is Sorrow, there is holy ground."

He also learned about forgiveness and repentance – but not in the Dorian Gray kind of way. You have to forgive, he said, and so pluck the bitterness out of the heart – "one cannot always keep an adder in one's breast to feed on one" – because only then can you become self-realised. Self-realisation, the becoming of a complete individual, he also saw as essential.

"The essence of thought, as the essence of life, is growth."

"Self-culture is the true ideal of man."

"Where self-development has ceased to be the ideal, the intellectual standard is instantly lowered and, often, ultimately lost."

"Behind everything that is wonderful stands the individual. It is not the moment that makes the man, but the man who creates the age."

Mechanical people know where they want to go – and go there – but those who seek self-realisation don't know where they're going and furthermore they never get there because each of us is a mystery and the soul is ultimately unknowable. "My nature is seeking a fresh mode of self-realisation. And the first thing I have got to do is free myself from any possibility of feeling against you," he wrote in his book-length letter to Bosie.

"The external things of life seem to me now of no importance at all. You can see to what intensity of individualism I have arrived, or am arriving rather for the journey is long."

Love too is vital. "Love is fed by the imagination, by which we become wiser than we know, better than we feel, nobler than we are: by which we can see Life as a whole: by which, and by which alone, we can understand others in their real as in their ideal relations. Only what is fine, and finely conceived, can feed Love. But anything will feed Hate." "Hate blinds people."

"At all costs," he said on being sent down, 'I must keep Love in my heart. If I go to prison without Love what will become of my soul?"

As for art, he gave up on Pater and came round to Ruskin's point of view. When we reach "true culture" we reach a perfection in which sin is impossible because nothing can then harm the soul, that 'divine entity' which has the power to make something rich, fine and new out of what to others would be "commonplace, ignoble, vile."

Whistler didn't think there was a connection between the decay of society and the decay of art because the artist is already so disconnected that the state of society can't effect him. "There never was an artistic period," Whistler said, "there never was an artistic nation." Wilde disagreed – the decay (and renewal) or art and society go together. "Aesthetics are higher than ethics."

"Even a colour sense is more important, in the development of the individual, than a sense of right and wrong."

"Ethics make life possible. Aesthetics make life lovely and wonderful, and give progress, variety and change."

"Music creates for one a past of which one has been ignorant, and fills one with a sense of sorrows that have been hidden from one's tears."

We'd weary of the world "if Art did not purify it for us, and give to it a momentary perfection."

Rhyme has a "spiritual element of thought and passion." Art is spiritual in the sense that it can uplift and sanctify. Machines make men into machines, artists make men into artists. When it came to beauty, as well, I think he saw that art for the sake of art isn't enough – it has to be for the sake of something better, and for a Platonist that something is Being. Plato, Wilde said, was the first to feel "the desire to know the connection between Beauty and Truth."

"Truth in Art is the unity of a thing with itself: the outward rendered expressive of the inward: the soul made incarnate: the body instinct with spirit. For this reason there is no truth comparable to Sorrow."

"What the artist is always looking for is that mode of existence in which soul and body are one and indivisible."

Modern landscape painting showed a "subtlety and sensitiveness of impression, its suggestion of a spirit dwelling in external things and making its raiments of earth and air, of mist and city alike." (Which answers Gauguin's strictures on Impressionism.)

"Far off, like a pearl, one can see the City of God. It is so wonderful that it seems as if a child could reach it in a summer's day. One can realise a thing in a single moment, but lose it in the long hours that follow with leaden feet. It is difficult to keep the 'height that the soul is competent to gain.' We think in Eternity, but we move slowly through Time."

He agreed with Plato on education: the child should be so brought up that "the beauty of material things may prepare his soul for the reception of the beauty that is spiritual." Plato said: "Love of beauty is the true aim of education." Doing so leads a person automatically to choose the good over the bad.

He even sided with Ruskin – without saying so – over Gothic architecture. The Gothic gave us Chartres, Arthurian legends, St Francis, Giotto, Dante. The Renaissance gave us Petrarch, Raphael, Palladianism, French tragedies, St Paul's, Pope's poetry "and everything made from without and by dead rules, and does not spring from within though some spirit informing it".

And, finally he spoke like a true Platonist: "Still, I am conscious now that behind all this Beauty there is some Spirit hidden of which the painted forms and shapes are but modes of manifestation, and it is with this Spirit that I desire to become in harmony. The Mystical in Art, the Mystical in Life, the Mystical in Nature. It is absolutely necessary for me to find it somewhere."

Not that, once freed, he ever did. Out of jail, he crossed to France and then into Italy and soon went back to his old ways – with Bosie for a while, though Bosie deserted him when things got bad. He may, or may not, have converted to Catholicism on his death bed. It was something he seems to have wanted to do, off and on, most of his life: once, when he was a young man, he was on the point of doing so until his father said he'd lose his allowance if he did. (Oddly enough his chief tormentor – the Marquess of Queensberry, Bosie's father – did convert on *his* death bed. While still an atheist he'd asked to be buried without a coffin – "earth to earth" –

in any place "where the stars shall shed their light, and sun shall gild its rising morn". Who'd have thought the half mad, furious and ferocious old man had such poetry in him?)

Near his own end, Wilde said: "why is it that one runs to one's ruin? Why has destruction such a fascination?" He never gave an answer – a pity, since it might have given us an insight into the self-destructive urges and rages of today's middle classes. (What would he make of *them*, given his contempt for their great-great-grandfathers?)

One morning just before he died Wilde met a friend of his mother in the Champs-Elysées. Why didn't he write any more? "Because I have written all there is to write. I wrote when I did not know life, now that I know the meaning of life, I have no more to say."

Why did Aestheticism fail? You can see why by comparing Wilde's final belief in Beauty as redemptive and mystical with Whistler's opinions on art. Whistler, an aesthete who denied he'd ever been one, described Aestheticism like this: "Art should stand alone and appeal to the artistic sense of eye and ear, without confounding this with emotions entirely foreign to it, as devotion, pity, love, patriotism." Not so, said Wilde the Platonist: beauty connects Becoming to Being. Love, said Plotinus, is nothing more than a response to beauty. Beauty is a means, never an end.

Whether Wilde had mystical experiences is hard to tell. He did say to a lecturer in Nebraska University: "I was never touched by anything not tangible and visible but once, that was just before writing *Ave Imperatrix*". Wilde was twenty-seven when it wrote it. He was forty-four when he got out of jail, and then the 'Spirit behind Beauty' seems to have eluded him. He'd gone from a blend of un-socialist socialism and hedonism to Platonism and back to a mindless collapse. In a way he can stand in for the up-dated West a hundred years later. For Wilde there was no way back: is there one for the West?

CHAPTER THIRTEEN

Berkeleyan Immaterialism

A man said: "I see particular horses, not horseness." "That," replied Socrates, "is because you see with your eyes and not your soul."

Immateriality – what the soul sees (uncreated eternity and eternal Abstractions) – is at the heart of Platonism. But, although the Greeks knew all about the immaterial, they were ignorant of immaterialism – defined as: thought is primary, matter exists only in a mind. But immaterialism can add to and simplify Platonism: Bishop Berkeley (1685-1753), who is usually called the first immaterialist, is therefore one of the very few people who can both update and clarify the 'holy philosophy'. People get Berkeley wrong, as Dr Johnson did when he kicked a stone to prove that matter exists outside the mind. But Berkeley never said you wouldn't break your toe if you kicked a brick – he said you'd feel the pain in your mind. You see the stone inside your head and you feel the stone as well as the pain inside there also. Even materialists agree this is true. Look at a mountain and you see it inside your head. Photons are reflected from the snowy peak above the timberline, pass into the eye, are converted into electro-chemical signals which are then carried into the brain and turned into an image of the mountain. You see inside your head. That being so, said Berkeley, how do you know the hills exist outside? You can never step outside to look.

Sir James Jeans put it this way: an atomic eruption in the sun sends out a photon which eight minutes later enters a poet's eye. So far there's been an unbroken chain of material cause and effect until the poet thinks non-physical, immaterial, 'poetic thoughts about the sunset'. It's matter all the way until the immaterial poetry comes along. Jeans also put it this way: Z is the eruption, Y is the photon flying free, X is its passage through space, and so on down through the alphabet until C (optic nerve), B (brain) and then a full-stop followed by A (immaterial thought). All science from quantum physics to biology has the same outcome – it's matter all the alphabetical way until A (non-matter).

Descartes said there are therefore two worlds, mind and matter, which never meet (which is really only Plato's Becoming and Being updated for the 17th century). Matter and thought, Descartes went on, are just too different to interact. True, said Berkeley, but the fact is they do interact so they must be the same thing and since they clearly aren't both matter, they must both be thought. Thought has to be in a mind and that mind is certainly not ours, so whose is it? Berkeley put it this way in his *Principles of Human Knowledge*: "All the choir of heaven and furniture of the earth, in a word all those bodies that compose the mighty structure of the world, have no existence outside a mind; for them to exist is for them to be perceived or known; consequently so long as they aren't actually perceived by (i.e. don't exist in the mind of) myself or any other created spirit, they must either have no existence at all or else exist in the mind of some eternal spirit; because it makes no sense – and involves all the absurdity of abstraction – to attribute to any such thing an existence independent of a spirit."

"To be convinced of this," Berkeley goes on, "you need only to reflect and try to separate in your own thoughts the existence of a perceptible thing from its being perceived – you'll find that you can't."

Berkeley called his philosophy 'immaterialism', others persist in re-naming it 'subjective' or 'empirical idealism': that is, it's a synthesis of empiricism (all you know are experiences in the mind which come in through the senses) and idealism (matter doesn't exist, only mental things do). It's subjective because each person knows it only personally and subjectively from within.

These seem to be facts, if not irrefutable at least not yet

refuted and we part company with Berkeley only when it comes to abstractions – the Bishop didn't believe in them because, as an empiricist, he thought of things as ideas or pictures and an abstraction is neither, and so can't be held in a mind. He was also distrustful of Newton, thinking he'd raised Abstractions, such as gravity, to the point where God could be nudged aside, and in that he was right. Newton worried about it, too.

Plato's Ideas, in fact, *are* Abstractions – numbers, codes, rules, maths, laws of physics, the ultimate values of goodness, truth, beauty. William Ralph Inge (1860-1954), the Platonist Dean of St Paul's, called them the Ultimate Values of Beauty, Love, and Wisdom. There can be no Nothingness because the Abstractions are always there. (Inge, incidentally, was nicknamed the Gloomy Dean because he, too, thought the West was crashing down in ruin.) From Berkeley, therefore, we just take the astonishing idea of immaterialism – matter doesn't exist, not in a free-standing way, independent of a mind. In his first *Dialogue* he has Philonous (lover of mind) say to Hylas (matter) that immaterialism solves many "a Mystery and Riddle" and in that he was right. If you're instinctively drawn to a Platonism of Being and Abstractions, then immaterialism explains most elegantly how these things can be. We merely have to update Plato by calling Being 'Consciousness", the only thing we can be sure of knowing.

We can imagine, then, how things might work: the Abstractions cannot *not* be, they don't need matter, they don't need consciousness. But what if the Abstractions are like Aristotle's Potential which *have* to be actualised and, when actualised, become Consciousness? Without Consciousness, the Abstractions are incomplete and that can't be. Likewise, consciousness would be incomplete without cosmic matter. (So would the cosmos vanish if the Thinker dozed off? The Abstractions would surely wake the sleeper and get things back to normal.) Like a good many things, this isn't all that new: the Neo-Platonism of Plotinus – the descending of the immaterial One down through Mind

129

into Soul and so into matter – is very similar.

Similar but not the same because we now have to take science into account: if science can't wear it, we have to be very wary about carrying on. So we can speculate – no more than that – that billions of years of evolution brought matter to a pitch of complexity which allows Consciousness to break through – to *im*-materialise, we could say – in the human brain. Consciousness now has another angle on things, which is perhaps the whole point, the reason for it all, because we're here to report back and in so doing complete the scheme of things through directly experiencing the matter which Consciousness, by its nature, has to imagine.

But science also suggests that this Greater Consciousness doesn't have to imagine every last photon, atom or molecule in the cosmos. It isn't like closing your eyes and imagining a coffee cup. All you need are the mathematical Forms or Abstractions along with the basic rules governing how matter has to behave. The rest is science. Sir James Jeans denied that this was Idealism. "The true label is, I think, 'mathematical'." Nor need there be, I should add, anything supernatural about any of this.

The lesser and the greater consciousness, in other words, is the same thing, the lesser being filtered through, and muffled by, imagined matter. Yet sometimes the muffle works loose enough for the lesser to return to its origins, recorded as a mystical experience, or those lesser daily sightings of the invisible through the visible.

Voltaire said: "uncertainty is an uncomfortable position. But certainty is an absurd one", although he seemed to be pretty certain when he said certainty is absurd. Mostly it is, of course – but there is *one* certainty and everything else should flow from it: we *can't* doubt the existence of thought or consciousness. We *have* to doubt matter. Nothing makes sense if matter is primary. How does it create thought? How does thought move matter? There just is no evidence. In fact, rather as atheists demand that other people do their thinking for them and prove the existence of a God, perhaps materialists should be told to demonstrate how and why matter is real.

If they're honest, even materialists have to admit they don't know what matter is. What is it they see or sense? We have Kant's word for it that they can't know: the whatever-it-is in the outside world is funnelled through the senses into the brain, like raw stuff being carried into a factory. Raw stuff is carried in and then brain-made into something quite different, at least as far as anybody knows, and who can disprove it? You can't walk outside the factory to check. We do know that our limited senses begin to break down at the edge of quantum physics, so we know for a fact that some aspects of matter are ultimately beyond our capacity to know, visualise or understand. We can't prove matter exists and, if it does, we can't know what it is. Occam's razor also therefore suggests consciousness is primary.

All the same, immaterialism is an idea which appeals only to a specialised few. Perhaps it's a natural outcome of introversion. Introverts live in two worlds – like Being and Becoming – and the immaterial side is not only more important but also more real. Immaterialism is the extreme introvert's default position. To deny it, for them at least, is to deny the nature of things.

So conditioned are we in the West to see nothing but matter that, even when convinced by reason, the ability to view the world from a new angle is hard, impossible at times. But the switch can be made and then it's a bit like looking at one of those drawings which are also optical illusions: two heads facing each other flick into a vase, or an old woman flips into a young one. Best of all is Jastrow's duck which turns into a rabbit: in the West, materialism is the default duck but it can flop over into the immaterialist rabbit and, once it does, nothing is ever the same again.

These ideas have been around for three centuries and have never been all the rage – in fact I can think of only four people who've admitted to being immaterialists: three are dead and I'm a bit long in the tooth. I also have doubts, from time to time, about the Bishop who, having had the idea in his early twenties didn't exactly spend his life proselytising – spent in fact an awful lot of time campaigning for tar water (pine resin) as a cure-all rather as we regard antibiotics and vitamin pills. Some people, reading his book, *Siris*, suggest he may have repented in his old age, though that may be wishful thinking and, in any case, wouldn't invalidate the idea.

The three principal non-living immaterialists are:

George Berkeley was Anglo-Irish, born metaphorically inside the Pale. He was fifteen at the turn of the 18th century and a student in Trinity College, Dublin. He graduated at nineteen, was ordained an Anglican priest at twenty-five (in 1710) by which time he'd published the book around which his name still revolves: *The Principles of Human Knowledge* – the immaterialist's handbook, except we don't acknowledge physical hands or material books. At the age of twenty-seven he was elected Junior Fellow of Trinity College and Senior Fellow ten years later, by which time he was in London where he was received in Queen Anne's court, mixed with Swift, Addison and Pope, and wrote articles for Richard Steele.

For eight years, between twenty-eight and thirty-six, he travelled in Europe, as a chaplain at one time, a chaperone at another. But, like Plato, he wanted to set up an ideal state. Unlike Plato, he had the American colonies where he could experiment with a Christian utopia: his ideas have been described as Christian socialism. To that end, he wanted to found a college in Bermuda to train his missionaries. He married when he was forty-four and he and his wife sailed to Rhode Island. They were there for three years (1728-31) until he realised the Government back home wasn't going to pay for his college. Farm, house and books were donated to Yale and Harvard. He also wrote *Alciphron* in Rhode Island: it was printed in London the year after they landed back in England. Back in England, he wrote seven books in three years, before becoming Bishop of Cloyne, in County Cork, at the age of forty-nine in 1734. At one time he'd been an absent Dean of Derry but as a bishop he was active, helping both Protestants and Catholics. He was Bishop for nineteen years and died in Christ Church, Oxford, where he and his wife had gone to settle their son into the college. He was sixty-eight and by his own request remained unburied until he was quite clearly dead and decaying (people were sometimes buried alive, only to come to in the grave and die a terrible death underground).

Sir James Jeans (1877-1946) was a physicist and mathematician known, in circles where such things are known, for the Jeans Length or Jeans Instability which says that a cloud of interstellar gas with a radius less than the Jeans Length will fly apart, unable to collapse into a new star. He was also one of the duo who formulated the Rayleigh-Jeans Laws about black body radiation. Two of Jeans's hypotheses, however, fell with time: the steady-state universe and the belief that the planets were formed from material pulled from the sun by a passing star. In 1931 he published a book, *The Mysterious Universe,* about his immaterialism. In an interview with *The Observer* he said: 'I incline to the idealistic theory that consciousness is fundamental, and that the material universe is derivative from consciousness, not consciousness from the material universe. In general the universe seems to me to be nearer to a great thought than to a great machine."

The science in the first four chapters of his book has dated, badly in some cases, but the immaterialist conclusions in the fifth have never, as far as I know, been refuted. Even so, Jeans was very careful to qualify everything he said – quite rightly: in the end we don't know.

A A (Arthur Ashton) Luce (1882-1977), Professor of Philosophy at Trinity College, Dublin, was a Gloucestershire boy who awarded the Military Cross as an officer in the Royal Irish Rifles in the Great War (he'd been a student at Trinity). With T E Jessop he edited the Bishop's complete works (in nine volumes, 1948-1957) and became a Berkeleyan immaterialist himself. He was also the first, I think, to point out that Berkeley owed a lot to Nicholas Malebranche (1638-1715). Malebranche played with the idea that the things of the world are nothing more than ideas in God's mind, but retreated into dogma (he was a monk in Paris) for comfort and safety. Berkeley, an Anglican priest, was more open to the idea. They may have met. In 1943 – while Snell was working on the evolution of consciousness in Hamburg – Luce crossed to London from Dublin to give a lecture on Berkeley to the British Association. Luce was also a chess-playing fly fisherman whose motto was "fishing and philosophy: trout and truth". In his book, *Sense without Matter*, he wrote: "Descartes and Malebranche have weighed matter in the balance of reason and found it wanting. They have tried to fit it into their theories of perception and have failed. Does matter exist? They asked the question and burked the answer."

Luce blamed Aristotle for matter. The Philosopher took an old word, *hyle,* which once meant wood (firewood originally, I believe) and used it to mean what we now call matter. In this way he taught the West something false and damaging because it doesn't exist. The Romans followed the same route – their word for firewood had been *materia,* which is our word 'matter', of course. (*Hyle* survives in the English word 'hylozoism' but modern Greek, I understand, has lost it.)

All of this is all very well, of course, but what use is it to a declining West? In his own lifetime, Berkeley's great idea was either ridiculed, scorned or just avoided out of politeness. As already said, it appeals to a minority of a minority of a certain type of temperament and for them the concept is not only irrefutable but also of infinite value. All the same, the idea can be put to use in a more concrete way.

CHAPTER FOURTEEN

A Two-Legged West?

Christianity has always been evolutionary – it was a long time, for example, before all Christians accepted that Jesus was God. Neither Matthew, Mark nor Luke thought so. That St Paul did is disputable. The first Christians were Jews who never dropped their Jewish customs. Mid-way through the 2nd century, St Justin Martyr remarked that even then not everybody accepted it. A hundred years later Origen was claiming that Christ was a created soul like the rest of us, just better than we are. But, a hundred years after that, saying such a thing led to upheaval in the Greek-speaking end of the world when Arius (250–336), a priest in Alexandria, also argued that Christ was created. The Arian and anti-Arian uproar which followed led to the Ecumenical Council of Nicaea, near Constantinople, in 325 and the first attempt to formulate a Christendom-wide doctrine, and then only under political pressure from the Emperor, Constantine, who sat in purple robes on a gold throne looking down on the clerics. (The Bishop of Rome sent two priest-observers.) The meeting of just over two hundred bishops voted that the Father and Son *is*, in fact, God: they share the 'same-being' or *homo-ousios*.

The meeting balked, however, at including the Paraclete in a fully equal Trinity and, in fact, the Council had really only been called to get of Arianism and establish, once and for all, Christ's divinity. But was the Holy Spirit divine or created? An outline of a Trinity had been there since the end of the 1st and the beginning of the 2nd centuries when the Fourth Gospel was written. St John stressed the presence of the Holy Spirit and at the same time believed that Jesus was God. Theologians also claimed that the Trinity was there in

135

embryo in *Genesis* since God/the Word/the Spirit had created the heavens and the earth. In the 4th century, when so much was settled, the Cappadocian Fathers pressed the divinity of the Holy Spirit, quoting St Matthew's Gospel: people were baptised in the name of the Father, Son and Holy Ghost. The issue was settled in the Council of Constantinople in 381. Meanwhile, the contents of the New Testament were agreed by the end of the 4th century and haven't changed since. On the other hand, it wasn't until the Council of Chalcedon, across the Bosporus from Constantinople, in 451 that the dual nature of Christ, 'perfect God and perfect man', was established. The Athanasian Creed defining the Trinity was probably written in the 5th or 6th century, on the edge of the Dark Ages.

In other words, Christianity evolved, slowly. Its evolution, in the West at least, has never stopped. Scholasticism was an attempt to widen the faith with Greek philosophy. The Reformation was an undoing of evolution, in some ways. In the 20th century – to take an example at random – Rudolf Bultmann (1884-1972) wanted to replaced the old, no longer believable, myths in the Bible with new ones.

What saved Christianity in the beginning was probably its hellenisation – it had in fact been *lightly* hellenised from its beginning, as had been the Judaism of the diaspora (outside Judaea and Jerusalem, that is). The Septuagint had already been translated into Greek and Philo of Alexandria (20 BC-50 AD) was really a Helleno-philo. St Luke was Greek, while St Paul came from Greek-speaking Tarsus ('no mean city') which was a stronghold of Stoicism. In his *The Authority of the Bible*, C H Dodd maintained that St Paul took at least three ideas from Stoicism: the concept of conscience, the laws of nature, and the need for self-sufficiency.

All the same, Christianity had a long way to go. In *Pagan and Christian in an Age of Anxiety,* E R Dodds suggested that, even in the 2nd century, educated pagans would have pointed to its biggest and most basic flaw – pagans went in for 'reasoned conviction', Christians for 'blind faith': for *logismos* not *pistis*, the difference between the Jewish and Greek way of thinking. St Paul "represented *pistis* as the very foundation of Christian life." "What astonished all the early pagan observers," Dodds wrote, "was the Christian's reliance on unproved assertion – their willingness to die for the indemonstrable". Celsus said Christians were "the enemies of science". The new Platonised Christianity, however, changed all that. *Pistis,* said Origen, is for the many since 'very few people are enthusiastic about rational thought': *logismo* is for the few who are.

In the late 2nd century, as well, Clement of Alexandria (c150-c215) argued in his book, *Stromata,* that Christians had to stop being afraid of philosophy ("as children fear scarecrows") and engage with it otherwise their religion would be nothing more than a cult for the uneducated. (At the same time, he added that it was pointless trying to prove that God exists: Christianity is about revelation, not analysis. Belief comes when you make your mind up to have faith.) In other words, balance the Platonist wing of consciousness with the Aristotelian.

Not everybody agrees that the hellenisation was either deliberate or deep, and many early Christians rejected it outright – even as late as the 5th century, Nestorius said people were being 'led astray by the mentality of the Greeks', and he was Archbishop of Constantinople at the time, although later expelled and exiled as a heretic. Jaroslav Pelikan in *The Emergence of the Catholic Tradition* wrote: "Taken as it stands, 'hellenisation' is too simplistic and unqualified a term for the process that issued in orthodox Christian doctrine. Nevertheless, it is true that in its language and sometimes in its ideas orthodox Christian doctrine still bears the marks of its struggle to understand and overcome pagan thought." But hellenised it was and not only by taking over the tools of logic and thought developed by the philosophers. Pelikan, for example, agreed that the "idea of the immortal and rational soul is part of the Greek inheritance". The 'impassibility' of God – as opposed to the rages and wrath of Jehovah – is also Greek. He also quoted Tertullian (c160-c225), the first of the Latin-language theologians: "What has Athens to do with Jerusalem?" Tertullian asked. "Quite a lot," he could have answered. He himself adopted the Stoic soul, a thing made of very fine matter, rather perhaps like our energy. (His God was also made of matter.) Pelikan also quoted Gregory of Nyssa (c335-c395) who insisted that "we make Sacred Scripture the rule and norm of every doctrine" – yet, because he was a mystic, couldn't escape the *Phaedo*.

Justin Martyr (100-165) said he was led to Christianity by the philosophers – the Stoics, Aristotle, Pythagoras, Plato, in that order. None was quite right and he was converted in an afternoon by an old man he met on the sea shore. Justin identified Plato's The Good with the Biblical God, quite wrongly (they have little in common), and pointed to Socrates as the way Christian martyrs should behave. Plato said that finding your way to God is hard: Justin agreed – it *can* be done but not without the Paraclete. From Stoicism he took the idea of Logos or divine Reason and claimed it had inspired the Jewish Prophets and (as Henry Chadwick put it) "was present entire in Jesus Christ". Implicit in Justin, Chadwick went on in *The Early Church*, is the idea that God is transcendent but Christ is immanent in the form of the Logos, the only way God and the material world can meet. Furthermore, said Justin, the Son is 'derived' from the Father as one torch is lit from another (no hint there of the Holy Spirit as part of a Trinity).

In the very early days, as well, it was easier for Christians to borrow from philosophy because their dogmas and doctrines hadn't yet been set in stone. In *De Principiis,* Origen accepted most of the Platonist theology including the world-soul, the idea that the cosmos is alive and suffused with reason, thought or mind. The stars also had souls and were the destinations of the saved. People, in fact, got there after many incarnations in which the soul learned, little by little, what was good for it. (Reincarnation was condemned as heretical only in 543 when the Emperor, Justinian (c482-565), said it was.) Post-mortem punishment was more like medication – to cure, not to hurt. Hell was not a place but a 'state of mind' caused by a lack of wholeness of the soul. (Hell wasn't widely believed in, anyway.) For Origen, E R Dodds said, "Heaven is an endless university" – and, since Dodds was Regius Professor of Greek in Oxford, he may even have thought this a good thing. As they pass their exams, souls will be given bodies which are progressively more and more aetherial until they're finally freed of all matter, however attenuated and gossamer.

More usefully for today, Origen saw the Bible texts as allegories, sometimes with four layers of meaning, but this also he'd taken from the Greek custom of explaining passages of Homer – Celsus and Porphyry both detected Platonism in *The Iliad* and *The Odyssey*. Better than allegory, perhaps, is Origen's idea that these stories can have both literal and spiritual meanings, a bit like Plato's myths of the Cave, Er and so on.

In Western Christianity, St Augustine (354-430) was the key hellenising figure. Platonism to him was "the most pure and bright of all philosophy." He also said that the Incarnation was the only bit of Christianity which he didn't find in Platonism but in that he was wrong: the concept of a Creator God is wholly Judaic, not in the least Greek. The Forms now existed in God's mind and so were no longer primary and eternal – they were created specifically to inform or shape matter, like templates, moulds or patterns. Numbers are Forms which rule matter. St Augustine also had a theory of evolution – the Abstractions in the shape of numbers were seeded in matter to germinate when the time was ripe, hence, the timing of Christ's birth. The Abstractions – particularly the Good, the Truth and Beauty – illuminate our minds because they are the eternal truth of God. The earthly world is unstable and changing, knowable only imperfectly through our uncertain senses: the spiritual world is knowable with perfect clarity without them. Because people are made in

God's image, they, too, can know these eternal things directly through grace, by-passing the senses. St A himself turned inward to the inner immaterial reality, away from the external and material. It was in ways like these that he Christianised basic Platonist ideas.

We're familiar with St Augustine's insight that time isn't eternity – it isn't the everlastingness of the Middle Platonists – but was created with the universe. "Non in tempore, sed cum tempore, finxit Deus mundum." 'God made the the world not in time but at the same time as time.' As so often, however, Plato got there first. In the *Timaeus* he wrote: "Time and the heavens came into being at the same instant, in order that, if they were ever to dissolve, they might be dissolved together. Such was the mind and thought of God in the creation of time."

As Christian spread, paganism mounted a surprisingly feeble rear-guard action. There were persecutions under one or two Emperors (Diocletian (244-31), for example) as matters of political policy: Nero's seems to have been a cover-up for his own crime of arson. Less well know is the fact that a few philosophers hit back as well. Celsus (2nd century) wrote a book called *The True Word* which has been lost but which we know about from Origen's rebuttal – a kind of old time frisking – in *Paracelsus*. What follows is taken mainly from Henry Chadwick's *Christian Thought and the Classical Tradition*. Celsus, to begin with, was a Middle Platonist and polytheist who thought the lesser deities were localised aspects of the one God. He rejected the idea that some Greeks had had a kind of subliminal celestial tip-off about Christian truths centuries before Christ was born. Or – worse – that Plato had read and plagiarised Moses: it was much more likely, he said, that Jesus had read Plato, that Paul had read Heraclitus or that the New Testament was written by people steeped in Greek thought (which is largely true). Since the Greeks came first, Christianity had, logically, to be a corruption of Greek ideas. Noah's Flood, for example, is a copy of Deucalion's.

(His logic often let Celsus down.) Worse, Christianity was hostile to Greek reasoning: Christians didn't question, just dumbly believed – most, in fact, were stupid: ask them about the Resurrection and they just say 'everything is possible in God'.

Besides, Celsus went on, what Christians now preach Plato had taught five hundred years ago – humility, non-resistance to evil, that wealth stops you living the good life, that heaven is where good souls end up, and that divine and human wisdom are not the same. (Unable to refute this, Origen came up with a nice phrase – 'Christians cook for the multitude': Plato 'spiced the same dish to please the gentry'.) Christianity is also a broken branch of Judaism. Judaism is at least national and traditional – this new cult is neither and nothing can be both new and true.

Then Celsus got to the core of what is wrong: the misconception of a Creator-God: worse, this one is an interfering monster who created a world ten thousand years ago all for the sake of a few tribes of nomads in a desert, while the rest of us shall burn forever. Then he gets himself born as a baby in the back end of nowhere and starts ordering peasants around? It's all too childish. *And* he can't leave things alone and then, when he does barge in, everything goes wrong. He made evil, made people imperfect, and then runs around killing all and sundry because of the flaws he built into them in the first place. Monstrous. And the cruelty of it – death by drowning in floods, incineration by blazing brimstone, being turned into columns of salt. *And* he does all this because he feels neglected, disrespected? 'People ought to treat Me better,' he grouches. It's all too childish for words. Then there's an Incarnation. Impossible. If it happened, God must have changed and that can't be squared with being a perfect Being and how stupid is it that Christians think they won't be able to see their God after death unless they're given new eyes?

Celsus also accused Christians of brainwashing pagan children and turning them against their parents, something which Origen couldn't deny. But Celsus also grumbled that church music was so disturbingly beautiful it derailed all criticism.

The Emperor Julian (331-363) wrote a tract, *Contra Galilaeos* (Against the Galileans), a year before he died. He'd been brought up as a Christian and so knew their ways but was still as literal minded as any modern day atheist. Why did God create Eve when He must have know what she'd be like? Nobody had prophesied a virgin birth. Why did God suddenly go global after thousands of years spent fretting over a single desert tribe? But it was a bit late for counter-Christian arguments: a century earlier Porphyry (234-c305), had already despaired – Jesus was replacing Asclepius and churches were being built in villages let alone cities. Porphyry was also more scholarly: he knew Hebrew and so was able to prove that typology – the idea that some people in the Old Testament were secret signposts pointing to Christ's coming – was false.

Celsus and Julian were on the losing side as Porphyry realised. By the end of the 4th century, the Emperor Theodosius had decreed that Nicene Christianity was the official state religion. Why did Christianity win? The breakdown and the breakup of the Empire to begin with. Also "Paganism," as Dodds wrote, "had lost faith both in science and in itself". Society was collapsing, real Barbarians were at the gates and breaking through the frontiers, there were civil wars, swarming refugees, endemic disease, plague, inflation, hunger, uncertainty and unutterable loneliness. Plotinus saw people as puppets, rather than players, jerked about on unseeable strings. The outer world is not for us, only the inner. Cities are sacked, men massacred, women raped but, in the end, these are only passing things: there'll be new cities and perhaps the children "conceived in crime", as Dodds put it, "will prove better men than their fathers". Nothing's more to be said, Plotinus implied, about this terrible place where we have to live if only for a little while.

This giving-in infected Christians as well. Gregory of Nyssa (335-395), a mystic like Plotinus, compared all we do to children making castles out of damp sand. St Augustine shared these opinions. Too many people saw themselves as 'bags of excrement'. "Only the sick in soul," said Porphyry, "need Christianity" but of course most people were, and are. Positively, the church offered solace, a place to belong, help in sickness, food if you were hungry, companionship for the lonely. The Church was also both inclusive and inflexible – all welcome: sign up or be damned. In other words, it helped you in Becoming and helped you into Being.

It also preserved pagan civilisation in its monasteries until the dark times passed even while destroying it on the ground, sometimes with violence. Paladas, the Alexandrian poet of the bitterness of change, lived all his life within the 4th century, from the time Christianity was sorting itself out until it was on top. He probably lived to see the destruction of temples licensed unofficially by Theodosius in 391 but not to witness the death of Hypatia, daughter of his own protector, Theon. Hypatia was a mathematician (a geometer) and astronomer, a Neo-Platonist who gave public lectures on Platonism. In 415 there were riots in Alexandria between Jews and Christians. Monks swarmed into the city to back Bishop Cyril. Among their victims was Hypatia – stripped of her clothes and stripped of her flesh down to her bones with oyster shells.

Paladas may not have seen that particular atrocity but he saw enough of his own. His poetry is sometimes pitiful in defeat, sometimes morosely bitter, at others self-comforting with Stoicism, Epicureanism and fatalism. He was a schoolmaster, which meant making children memorise whole passages of Homer, and as such was poor all his life. Here are parts of four of his poems, translated by Tony Harrison. In the first, Christians have pulled down a statue of Heracles and the poet is appalled: that night, however, the god ...

> ... stood at my bed-end
> and smiled and said: 'I can't complain,
> the winds of change are blowing, friend,
> and your god is just a weather-vane.

On a Temple of the Goddess Fortune Turned into a Tavern

> *... goddess once, and now a barmaid*
> *Is not too drastic a change of trade.*
> *You'll do nicely where you are*
> *behind the counter of* The Fortune Bar.

In a third poem:

> *The blacksmith's quite a logical man*
> *to melt an Eros down and turn*
> *the God of Love into a frying pan,*
> *omething that can also burn.*

On Monks

> *Solitaries? I wonder whether*
> *real solitaries live together?*

Like today, the changing world of Late Antiquity had no real spiritual base, just a welter of shallow gods, often barbaric: the official state gods, and the more alien ones – Attis and Cybele, Isis, Sol Invicta, the Gnostics, Mani, Mithras. Nor were the religious philosophies of the educated good enough to cope with the prevailing malaise: Stoicism seemed to inspire only the stern and unbending but with no comfort on offer. Cynicism was for hippies and drop-outs, Epicureanism for hippies who washed.

Platonism, on the other hand, had – and has – a lot going for it as a religion or religious way of life, superior in many ways – but not, apparently, in the ones that count – to Christianity. It begins with the Socratic question: 'How should we live?' Get that right and the answer to 'What's it all about?' appears automatically at the periphery. At the heart of Platonism is the insight that the eternal can be reached through the temporal with the help of Beauty which is an aspect of the Good which in turn is at the core of all right-action, right-thinking and decency. Plato said we belong to eternal Being: we come from there and want to get back. Abstractions or Ideas are also eternal and would exist even in a void, except there can't be a void since they're never not there. We can view them as the laws of nature, the codes governing the way things are, numbers and maths. Redness is a concept which would still exist abstractly even if all red things vanished from the earth, or if the cosmos ended. Beauty, Truth and the Good are also Abstractions.

Platonism has a moral code as well. Wrong-doing is wrong, always: don't do it – apart from anything else, it makes you smaller when the point of life is growth. Be open to ideas but not uncritically: question everything. A government's job is to hold a space open for the intellectual and spiritual expansion of each individual. Live by the rule of law but don't make laws to change human nature, instead teach decency and don't just threaten those who haven't been so taught with the jailhouse.

The problem with Platonism, however, is its unpopularity – it's too abstract and esoteric, too rarefied to appeal to many, having no rituals, priests, or altar-like or pulpit-like points of focus. Within two hundred years of Plato's death, it had evolved into something mechanical and exoteric. Middle Platonism lasted from the beginning of the 1st century BC to the 2nd century AD. Plutarch (46-120 AD) is the best know of them. A H Armstrong summed up the beliefs of a typical Middle Platonist in this way: he had a 'remote intellectual devotion to the remote Supreme' whom (or which) he hoped to see in the next life, and occasionally in this: below the Supreme Mind is a Second Mind and below that a swarm of daemons and lesser gods, including the sacred stars. Between them they keep the World Soul, which is the visible universe, in being and in working order. More importantly, Middle Platonism attested that the soul is divine and the aim of life is to purify it through philosophy so that, after death, it will see the Supreme in Eternity, by which was meant everlastingness. Celsus, who was a Middle Platonist, may have had a mystical experience which he attributed to the same Supreme.

Neo-Platonism in the hands of Iamblicus (250-325) and Proclus (412-485) fell into ruin, dwindled into a thing of sorcery and spells, although they seemed to think it might be a buffer against Christianity, a way of bringing pagan cults together. It was partly based on Plato's *Timaeus* and *Parmenides*, but also on the *Chaldean Oracles* which had been handed down by the gods. The strangest of their ideas must be The Henads, or The Ones. Ones in the plural because there were millions of them, each a One, each a god. The aim was to rise to the supreme One through a system which was astonishingly hierarchical but through which you could step up only one grade at a time, and for that you needed magic.

So Platonism, it seems, can't be made collective enough to solve the shrinkage problem which leaves really only Christianity as a religious way of re-expanding it. But is Christianity up to it? Can it evolve yet again? It's had some very unlikely, very unsaintly, lay defenders whose arguments are more persuasive than those of most theologians – Oscar Wilde, for example. Jesus was one of the consolations he discovered in Reading Jail, though his Jesus was non-divine, a mortal man: if he were God "it would place too broad a gulf between him and the human soul". Wilde's Christ was cast in Wilde's own image – both turned their lives into works of art. Jesus was an artist, a forerunner of the Romantics, and his message was "Be Thyself", a step up from the Socratic "Know Thyself." All artists are extreme individualists and Christ is their apostle because he knew the secret of life lies in the individual soul and that the Kingdom of Heaven is within. The artist's life is therefore a guide to conduct, Wilde also said, though certainly not autobiographically.

Christ, in fact, 'ranks with the poets' and his life story is greater than the entire 'cycle of Greek Tragedy'. Nothing in all literature compares to the Passion: supper (with a betrayer), "anguish in the quiet moonlit olive-garden," a false friend to betray, a true friend to run away, loneliness, submission, acceptance, a magistrate washing away his own guilt, a "coronation of sorrow", crucifixion before his mother and the disciple he loved, soldiers dicing for his cloak, a terrible death (giving the world its most 'eternal symbol'), a

146

tomb, an empty tomb, resurrection. Nothing in art is remotely like it and only the imaginative can see it at all. The life of Christ is Sorrow and Beauty made one.

There *were* miracles and they came from 'the charm of his character' – bringing 'peace to souls in anguish', making the deaf hear the Voice of Love, the blind to see the Beauty which is love. "Evil passions fled at his approach." The multitude on the mountain were too engrossed to feel hungry. Water could taste like wine in his presence. Wilde also quoted Renan who, in his book *Vie de Jesus*, told us that love "was the lost secret of the world for which the wise had been looking, and that it was only through love that one could approach either the heart of the leper or the Feet of God".

"When one comes in contact with the soul," Wilde went on, "it makes one as simple as a child". To do so you have to ditch everything – possessions and passions and everything you've ever learned. Few meet the soul. "Most people are other people. Their thoughts are someone else's opinion, their life is a mimicry, their passions a quotation. Christ is not merely the supreme individualist but he was the first in History."

Not that that will do for today. The biggest stumbling block – *skandalon* or scandal – is the Creator-God idea. In other words, a spiritual dimension to balance the analytical one in the West is barely possible because the West's own religion militates against it.

But there are other ways of looking at it. We can, for example, argue rationally for the primacy of a Consciousness and we can (if we wish) call it God and, as Origen pointed out, the truth can be either literal or spiritual. What appears to be the literal truth can stay for those who want it. Others can look at Christianity from a Berkeleyan and Platonist, non-literal, non-supernatural point of view. God the Father is the Platonic Abstractions, the Ideas: the Holy Spirit is Consciousness: the Son is Consciousness re-emerging through created matter to reconnect with where it comes from. The Crucifixion and Resurrection show, symbolically, that Consciousness can't die.

Bibliography

Aquinas, St Thomas *Selected Philosophical Writings* (trans. Timothy McDermott) OUP, Oxford, 2008

Aristotle *The Basic Works of Aristotle* (ed. Richard McKeon) The Modern Library, New York, 2001

Armstrong, A H *An Introduction to Ancient Philosophy* Methuen, London, 1947

Barfield, Owen *Poetic Diction: a Study in Meaning* Barfield Press, Oxford, 2010

Barfield, Owen *Saving the Appearances: a Study in Idolatry* Wesleyan University Press, Middletown, Connecticut, 1988

Barzun, Jacques *From Dawn to Decadence* HarperCollins, New York, 2000

Berkeley, George *Alciphron* J Tonson, London, 1732

Berkeley, George *Philosophical Works* Everyman, London, 1992

Berkeley, George *Siris* Forgotten Books (facsimile edition), 2012

Blackmore, Susan *Consciousness: an Introduction* Hodder Education, London, 2010

Bloom, Allan *The Closing of the American Mind* Simon & Schuster, New York, 1987

Bloom, Harold *Shakespeare: the Invention of the Human* Fourth Estate, London, 1999

Booker, Christopher *The Real Global Warming Disaster* Continuum, London, 2010

Brown, Peter *The World of Late Antiquity* Thames and Hudson, London, 1971

Browne, Anthony *The Retreat of Reason* Civitas, London, 2006

Chadwick, Henry *Early Christian Thought and the Classical Tradition* OUP, Oxford, 1966

Chadwick, Henry *The Early Church* Penguin, London, 1993

Chesterton, G K *Orthodoxy* Popular Classics Publishing, 2012

Chesterton, G K *St Thomas Aquinas* Echo Library, Teddington, 2007

Clark, Kenneth *Civilisation* B BC, London, 1981

Copleston, F C *Medieval Philosophy* Harper & Brothers, New York, 1961

Dalrymple, Theodore *Not With a Bang But a Whimper: the Politics and Culture of Decline* Monday, London, 2009

Dalrymple, Theodore *Our Culture, What's Left of It* Ivan R Dee, Chicago, 2005

Dawkins, Richard *The God Delusion* Bantam Press, London, 2006

Delingpole, James *Watermelons: how environmentalists are killing the planet, destroying the economy and stealing your children's future* Biteback, London,2012

Dodd, C H *The Authority of the Bible* Fontana, London, 1962

Dodds, E R *Pagan and Christian in an Age of Anxiety* W W Norton, London, 1970

Ellmann, Richard *Oscar Wilde* Vintage Books, New York, 1988

Freeman, Charles *The Closing of the Western Mind: the Rise of Faith and the Fall of Reason* Pimlico, London, 2003

Grant, Michael (ed.) *Greek Literature: an Anthology* Penguin, London, 1976

Green, Ellen and Skinner, Marilyn B (editors) *The New Sappho on Old Age* Center for Hellenic Studies, Harvard, 2009

Gregory, John (translator) *The Neoplatonists* Kyle Cathie, London, 1991

Guthrie W K C *The Greek Philosophers* Routledge, London, 2012

Guthrie W K C *Socrates* CUP, Cambridge, 1986

Hannam, James *God's Philosophers: How the Medieval World Laid the Foundations of Modern Science* Icon, London, 2012

Harris, Frank *Oscar Wilde, His Life and Confessions* Panther, London, 1965

Hayek, F A *The Road to Serfdom* University of Chicago Press, Chicago, 2007

Hitchens, Christopher *god is not Great: How Religion Poisons Everything* Twelve, New York, 2007

Hitchens, Peter *The Rage Against God* Continuum, London, 2010

Inge, W R, *Mysticism in Religion* Rider & Co, London, 1969

Irwin, Terence *Classical Thought* OUP, Oxford, 1991

Jeans, Sir James *The Mysterious Universe* CUP, Cambridge, 1931

Johnson, Marguerite *Sappho* Bristol Classical Press, Bristol, 2007

Johnson, Paul *Intellectuals* HarperCollins, New York, 2007

Johnson, Paul *Socrates: a Man for Our Times* Viking Penguin, New York, 2011

Kimball, Roger *The Fortunes of Permanence: Culture and Anarchy in an Age of Amnesia* St Augustine's Press, South Bend, 2012

Kimball, Roger *The Rape of the Masters: How Political Correctness Sabotages Art* Encounter Book, San Francisco, 2004

Kirk, GS, Raven JE, Schofield, M *The Presocratic Philosophers* CUP, Cambridge, 1983

Kolakowski, Leszek *Main Currents of Marxism* W W Norton & Co, New York, 2008

Kristeller, Paul Oskar *Renaissance Thought and the Arts* Princeton UP, Princeton, 1990

Luce, A A *Immaterialism,* British Academy, London, 1944

Luce, A A *Sense without Matter or Direct Perception* Nelson, London, 1954

McGrath, Alister E *Christian Theology* Blackwell, Oxford, 1997

Paglia, Camille *Glittering Images: A Journey Through Art from Egypt to Star Wars* Pantheon, New York, 2012

Palladas *Palladas: Poems* (trans. Tony Harrison) Anvil Press, London, 1992

Pelikan, Jaroslav *The Christian Tradition: 1 The Emergence of the Catholic Tradition* University of Chicago Press, Chicago, 1975

Plato *Two Comic Dialogues: Ion and Hippias Major* (trans. Paul Woodruff) Hackett, Indianapolis, 1983

Plato *The Last Days of Socrates* (trans. Hugh Tredennick) Penguin, London, 1983

Plato *The Laws* (trans. Trevor T Saunders) Penguin, London, 2004

Plato *Phaedrus and Letters VII and VIII* (trans. Walter Hamilton) Penguin, London, 1981

Plato *The Republic* (trans. GMA Grube (revised CDC Reeve)) Hackett Publishing Company, Indianapolis, 1992

Plato *The Republic* (trans. Robin Waterfield) OUP, Oxford, 2008

Plato *The Symposium* (trans. Walter Hamilton) Penguin, London, 1983

Plato *Timaeus and Critias* (trans. Desmond Lee) Penguin, 1983

Plato *Timaeus and Crito* (trans. Robin Waterfield) OUP, Oxford, 2008

Plotinus *The Essential Plotinus* (trans. Elmer O'Brien) Mentor, New York, 1964

Rist, J M *Stoic Philosophy* CUP, Cambridge, 1980

St Augustine *The Confessions of St Augustine* Hodder and Stoughton, London, 1992

Sappho *Poems and Fragments* (trans. Josephine Balmer) Brilliance Books, London, 1984

Scruton, Roger *The Face of God* Continuum, London, 2012

Snell, Bruno *The Discovery of the Mind in Greek Philosophy and Literature* Dover, New York, 1982

Stanford Encyclopedia of Philosophy (online)

Sullivan, Dick *Counter-Cosmos*, Coracle, London, 2012

Sullivan, Dick *Undertones* Coracle, London, 2010

Tarnas, Richard *The Passion of the Western Mind* Pimlico, London, 1998

Vlastos, Gregory *Socrates: Ironist and Moral Philosopher* CUP, Cambridge, 1997

Ware, Timothy *The Orthodox Church* Penguin, London, 1997

Waterfield, Robin *Why Socrates Had to Die: Dispelling the Myths*

Faber and Faber, London, 2009

Wilde, Oscar *The Picture of Dorian Gray* Penguin, London, 1985

Wilde, Oscar *Plays, Prose Writings and Poems* Everyman, London, 1983

Wind, Edgar *Pagan Mysteries in the Renaissance* OUP, Oxford, 1980

Yates, Frances A *Renaissance and Reform: The Italian Contribution* Routledge and Kegan Paul, London 1983

Index

A

Abelard, Peter 99-101, 111
Academy – Ficino's 113-114, 115:
    Plato's 90, 91
Achilles 32
Addison, Joseph 132
Adonis 92
Aesthetic Movement 93, 117-118,
    126
aesthetics 62, 124
Agamemnon 32
Age of Reason 42, 62
Albigenses 103
Alexander the Great 49-50
Amalricians 69
Anactoria 92
Anaxagoras 81
Anaximander 81
Anaximenes 81
Ancren Riwle, The 108
Andre, Carl 66
Antin, Mrs Eleanor 66, 67
Aphrodite 30, 32, 33, 93, 111, 113,
    116
Apollo 34, 60, 86, 113, 116
Aquinas, St Thomas 28, 98, **102-
    106**, 109, 113
architecture 60, 110-111, 125
Arianism 135
Ariel 40
Aristarchus 50
Aristophanes 34
Aristotle: influence on Aquinas
    102-106: art 53: influence on
    Cicero 55: consciousness 24,
    28-29, 35, 82: early Christians
    138: *eudemonia* 24, 104: the
    Forms 53-54, 87: the gods 53:
    the Golden Mean 54:
    hypostases 53-54: Justin Martyr
    138: learning as way to the
    divine 52: logic 96-97:
    materialism/immaterialism **51-
    54**: maths 98: matter,
    invention of 134: the Middle
    Ages 96-100, 115: motion 107:
    mysticism 53: poetry and
    tragedy 62: Potential 54, 129:
    role of the State 54. 104:
    science for growth of the soul
    55: scientific revolution 114:
    the Transcendent 52:
    Unmoved Mover 57
Armory Show, The NY 64, 65
Armstrong, A H 145
Arnold, Matthew 52
Arts, the 32-33, 34, 52, 58-67, 95:
    purpose of 58, 59: haiku
    moods 59: sadness and repose
    59: inspiration 61-62
Artemis 32
Arts and Crafts Movement 15, 18
Asclepiades 51
Asclepius 142
Athanasian Creed 136
Athanasius of Alexander 108
Atheism 15, 16, 22, 28, 35, 55, 67,
    68-80, 125-126, 130, 142
Athena 32, 60, 85
Athenian Enlightenment 30, 34,
    49, 82, 111
Atthis 33
Attis 144
Aurelius, Marcus 56-57

B

Baby Boomers 18, 24
Bacchus 61
Bacon, Francis 70, 98
Bacon, Roger 70, 98
Barfield, Owen 12-13, 37, 43
Barlaam 109
Barzun, Jacques 10
Basil of Nyssa 108
Baudelaire, Charles 93

Behaviourism 44
Berkeley 28: on atheism 15, 70, 71-74: power through controlling the language 22: Bermuda 71, 132: 'Berkeleyan/immaterialist' Christianity 147: consciousness 45: immaterialism 28, 78, **127-129**: ideas ridiculed 134: Life 132-133: Sam Johnson 83-84, 127: long march through the institutions 22-23: Malebranche 133-134: reason for materialism explained 78: Rhode Island 71, 132: the zombie question 45
Big Bang 56
Black Death 97, 109
Blackmore, Susan 45
Block, Ned 47
Bloom, Alan 10-11
Bloom, Harold 36, 37-40, 43, 58
Boedecker, Deborah 94
Boehme, Jakob 118
Boethius 96
Booker, Christopher 27
books, price of in Athens 60
Bosie (Lord Alfred Douglas) 122, 123, 125-126
Bradlaugh, Charles 70-71
Bradley, Katherine 93-94
Bradwardine, Thomas 107
Briggs, Asa 15
Brown, Peter 36
Browne, Anthony 24
Browning, Robert 93
Brueghel 29
Bruno, Giordano 114
Bultmann, Rudolf 136
Burgess, Anthony 39-40
Buridan, John 108
Byzantium 96, 112, 113

C

Cadmus 34
Caliban 29, 40
Cappadocian Fathers, the 108, 109, 136
Carson, Rachel 25, 26
Celsus 139, **140-142**, 145
Chadwick, Henry 138, 140
Chalmers, David 44, 46
Chartres Cathedral 111-112, 125
Chesterton, G K 13, 102-104
Christianity: abandoned Greek origins 70: early attacks on 136, 139, 140-142, 145: Berkeley defends 15: Crucifixion 101, 147: further evolution? 146-147: evolutionary 77, **135-146**: not spread by force 76: hellenisation 136, 137, 138, 139: hesychasm 108-109: impact on paganism 142-143, 146: Incarnation 139, 139, 141: individualism 14: inherent non-violence of 74: Justin Martyr and philosophy 138: the classics as moral as 113: Nicaea/Nicene 135, 142: Greek Orthodoxy 77, 108,109: PC-ness and Christianity 75: Platonism deeper than 116: 14: proofs of existence of God 137: Reformation 116: Resurrection 141, 146, 147: about revelation, not reason 136, 137: rival to socialism 80: scientific revolution and 1108-109: sourness of 32: the Virgin Mary 101, 111, 142: Wilde on 146-147:

Christianity: The Trinity 53, 100, 108, 135, 136, 138, Christ 63, 75, 77, 80, 98, 104, 108, 109, 120, 135, 136, 138, 139, 140, 142, 146, 147: Jesus 108, 120, 135,

138, 140, 142, 146, 147: Holy
Spirit 135, 136, 138, 147:
Paraclete 135, 138
Churchland, Patricia 44
Cicero 55, 69, 72, 73
Clark, Kenneth 14, 21-22, 110,
111, 112, 116
Clemenceau, Georges 110
Clement of Alexandria 108, 137
Climate Change (see
Greenhouse Effect)
Climategate 27
Cloud of Unknowing, The 108
Club of Rome 26
Cluny Abbey 100, 110
Cologne 94, 103
Conceptual art 65-67
Communism 14,16, 18, 70 (pre-
Marx), 109
Constantine, Emperor 96, 135
Constantinople 96, 109, 135, 136,
137
Collectivism 10, 12, 13. 14, 27, 39
Condorcet, Marquis de 21

Consciousness: Being as 129:
changing again? 42: deepening
of 37: deeper c 110: c can't die
147: can't doubt c 130, 131:
diminished 21, 58, 67, 73, 80,
110, 116: Epicurus 52-53:
expanded by art 21, 24, 57, **58-
67**, 62, 63-64, 67, 95:
expanded c illuminates the
world 101: learning expands
101: evolution of from Homer
30-36, 37-40, 134: Forms create
c 129: c as God 53, 147:
immateriality of 98: c
immaterialised 130:
consciousness incomplete 129,
133: greater intensity of being
110: lesser and greater kinds
130: Love as consciousness of
beauty 89: Marxism can't

account for 19:
Nominalism/Realist as two
strands 97-98, 100: c as
primary 131, 147: root of
decline/narrowing of 28, 29:
Sappho 95: Science and **44-47**,
61, 98: Shakespeare changed
consciousness 37-40: as soul
98: spectrum of 105: The
Trinity as Consciousness 147:
The wrecking of Western c 13
Consciousness: Two strands 28,
30, 40, 42, 62, 78, 97, 104, 105,
106, 108, 112, 137: Platonist
strand 28, 29, 46, 62,78,
86,105, 108,109, 110, 137:
Aristotelian strand 28, 29, 30,
39, 63, 96, 100, 105, 106, 109,
137: Aquinas – meeting of the
two 105:
Constantinople 96, 109, 135 et
seq
Cooper, Edith 93-94
Copernicus 11, 37, 114
Copleston, Frederick (Father)
106
Creator-God 67, 69, 70, 76, 108,
139, 141, 147
Critical Theory 22
Cromwell, Oliver 75
Cubism 64
Cultural Determinism 23
Cultural Marxism 22, 23
Cupitt, Don 71
Cybele 144
Cynics, the 50, 56, 68, 144
Cyril, Bishop 143

D
Dadaism 63-64
Dalrymple, Daniel 11-12
Dante, Alighieri 51, 57, 69, 112,
113, 125
Dardanelles, the 50, 81
Dark Ages 29, 96, 136

Darwinism 75
Dawkins, Richard 74-75, 76, 77-79
Deconstructionism 28
Delingpole, James 25-26
Deucalion 140
Delphi 34, 60
Democritus 51
Dennett, Daniel 45, 46
Demeter 31
Descartes, René 128, 134
Dialectical Materialism 22
Dickens, Charles 67
Diderot, Denis 20, 70
Diocletian, Emperor 140
Diogenes Laertius 81
Dodd, C H 77, 136
Dodds, E R 136-137, 139, 142
Dominicans, Order of 103
Donne, John 67
Douglas, Lord Alfred see Bosie
Duchamp, Marcel 63

E
Eckhart, Meister 28, 108, 112, 118
Eliot, T S 63
Eleusinian Mysteries 52, 91
Empiricism 28, 69, 101,106, 112, 116, 128, 129
Enlightenment, the 20, 28, 41, 51, 109
Environmentalism 10, 19, 25-26
Epicurus 28, **48-52**, 55, 117, 143, 144
Erigena 28, 86, 96-97
Eros 12, 33, 89, 93, 95, 144
Euclid 13, 97
Eupalinos 50
Euripides 34, 35, 81
Euthyphro 92
Eve 142
Expressionism 63

F
Falstaff 39-40

Faulconbridge 38
Fauvism 64
Ficino, Marsilio 28, 112 et seq
Field, Michael 93-94
Forester, C S 58
Fortune (goddess) 144
Foucault, Michel 63
Florio, John 40
Freud, Sigmund 64
Freya 30
Friedman, Milton 14
Funtowicz, Silvio 27
Fulbert, Canon 100
Futurism 64

G
Gaia 25, 31
Galileo 11, 97
Gauguin, Paul 59, 124
Gibbon, Edward 27
Gilbert and Sullivan 117
Giotto 125
Glass, Philip 65
Gnostics 144
Global Warming (see Greenhouse Effect)
God (Christian) 12, 13, 19, 45, 69, 70-72, 74 et seq, 80, 86, 92, 95, 98, 99, 101, 103 et seq, 124, 129, 130, 134 et seq, 142, 146, 147
God (pre-Christian Greek) 52, 54, 56, 76, 82, 87, 89, 115
gods, the 26, 27, 30 et seq, 42, 48-49, 53, 68-69, 76, 82, 84, 86, 93, 95, 115, 116, 122, 143 et seq
Godwin, William 21
Goethe 42-43
Golden Mean 25, 54
Goldschmidt, Victor 91
Gothic Architecture 9,110, 125
Goths, the 96
Greek Orthodoxy 77, 108-109
Greene, Ellen 95
Greenfield, Susan 42, 45
Greenhouse Effect 25-26

156

Greens, the 25-26
Gregorian Chant 93
Gregory of Nyssa 108, 138, 142
Gregory of Palamas 109
Grenfell, Bernard Pyne 94
Grosseteste, Robert (Bishop) 98-99
Guthrie, W K C 82, 87

H
haecceity 101-102
haijins 59
Hagel, G W F 73
Hagia Sophia 111
Hales, Thomas de 108
Hall, Joseph 75
Hamlet 39
Hammeroff, Stuart 44-45
Hannam, James 107
Harmonia 34
Harrison, Tony 143-144
Hartley, David 41
Hayek, Friedrich von 13-14, 42
Héloïse 100, 111
Heracles 28
Heraclitean Fire 55
Heraclitus 53, 84-85, 87, 140
Hermeticism 114
Hestia 53
Hesychasm 108-109
Heytesbury, William 107
Hippias 84-86
Hirelings 69
Hitchens, Christopher 74, 75, 76-77, 78
Hitchens, Peter 16-18, 77, 80
Hobbes, John 69-70
d'Holbach, Baron 70
Holy Spirit 135, 136, 138, 147 (see also Paraclete)
Homer 9, 30, 31, 32, 33, 37, 42, 61, 92, 139, 143
d'Hondetot, Sophie 20
homoousios 135
Hopkins, G M 101-102

Horace 49, 51
Hornblower 58
Hugh of St Victor 98, 108
humanism (*umanista*) 112, 113
Hume, David 20, 36, 51, 70, 78
Hunt, Arthur S 94
Huysmans, Joris-Karl 119
Hylton, Walter 108
Hypatia 143
hypostasis 53, 54

I
Iamblicus 145-146
Ibsen, Henrik 9, 24, 41
Idealism 28, 73, 128, 130, 133
Iliad, the 32
Imagism 63
immaterialism 28, **126-134**
immateriality 43, 47, 49, 86, **81-91**
Impressionism 59
Industrial Revolution 116
Inge, W R Dean 52, 80, 129
Ion 92
Iona 110
Ionia 30, 92
inscape 102
instress 102
Islam 15, 24, 76, 103, 109

J
Jackson, Frank 45-46
Jagger, Mick 10
Jason 34
Jastrow's rabbit/duck 131
Jeans, Sir James 127-128, 133
Jessop, T E 133
Jesus Prayer, the 108
Johnson, Marguerite 94
Johnson, Paul 19
Johnson, Dr Sam 83-84, 127
Judaism 69, 76, 77, 135 et seq, 141
Judas 80
Julian, Emperor 142
Julian Calendar 99

157

Just War 104
Justinian, Emperor 139

K

Kallipolis 64, 89
Kant, Immanuel 62, 131
Kepler, Johannes 114
Kierkegaard, Søren 14, 118
King, Martin Luther 75
Kirk, Capt (Star Trek) 46
Kristeller, P O 62, 112

L

Lampsachus 50
Lanfranc, Archbishop 98
Larkin, Philip 64
Leibnitz, G W 91
Lenin, Vladimir 119
Leonardo da Vinci 99
Lewis, C S 37
Lewotin, Richard 79
Libet, Benjamin 61
Locke, John 51, 116
Logos 56, 138
Luce, A A 133-134
Lucretius 15, 49
Ludwig of Bavaria 106

M

Magritte, René 64
Malebranche, Nicolas 133-134
Mallarmé, Stéphane 59, 63
Malthus, Thomas Robert, Rev
    26
Mandeville, Bernard 73
Mani 144
Manichaeism 103
Mao, Zedong 22
Marcuse, Herbert 22
Materialism 9, 14, 22, 27, 28, 43,
    45, 46, 47, **48-57**, 70, 76, 79,
    80, 81, 92, 116, 127, 131, 132, 133
Maria, Walter de 66-67
Marthas 69, 88
Marx, Fred 41

Marx, Karl/Marxism 11,14, 16, 19,
    21-22, 23, 25, 28, 41, 51, 63, 64,
    65, 70, 73, 96, 116
Maurier, George du 117
Medea 34
Medici, Cosimo de 114
Medieval Warm Period 97
Memory (Muse) 34
Mendel, Gregor 75
Merton Calculators 107
Meslier, Jean 70
Middle Ages 13, 18, 34, 37, 66,
    96-109, 110-113, 115-116, 117,
    120
Middle Platonism 115-116, 140,
    145
Milton, John 95
minimalism 66
Mirandola, Pico della 112
Mithras 144
Modernism 27, 63, 64, 65
MOMA, NY 66
Mona Lisa 63
Mondrian, Piet 60
Monet, Claude 110
Montaigne, Michel de 40
Moody, Todd 45
Moral Law 104
Morris, William 15, 18-19
Moses 140
Mount Athos 108
Mount Tabor 109
Multi-culturalism 28
Munch, Evard 63
music 9, 10, 59, 64-65, 91, 94,
    124, 141-142
mysterians 44
mysticism 30: Aquinas and 105-
    106: Aristotle and 53: atheists
    and 71: Celsus and 145:
    Dawkins and 77-78: Eckhart
    and 112: Epicurus and 49: 14th
    century 108: Greeks and 76:
    Gregory of Nyssa 138, 142:
    Hesychasm 108-109: G M

Hopkins 101, 102: Hugh of St Victor 98: immaterialism and 130: Middle Platonism and 115; Orphism and 82: Personal Platonism 82: Plato and 64, 86, **87-91**,116: Plotinus and 116, 142: Pythagoras 82: Ruysbroeck 69: Shelley and 21: Stoicism and 56: Wilde and 125, 126

N

Nagel, Thomas 44, 79
Natural Law 104
Nazis 11, 13-14, 26, 30, 42
Necker Cube 45
Neo-Platonism 96, 103, 114, 129, 143, 103, 114, 129, 145-146 (see also Plotinus)
Neo-Romanticism 28
Nestorius 137
New Labour 23
Newton, Sir Isaac 11, 37, 70, 75, 116, 129
Nicaea 135, 142
Nicholas of Oresme 107-108
Nietzsche, Friedrich 51, 70
Noah's flood 140
Noble Cause Corruption 27
Nominalism 28, 97-98, 100, 106, 109
North, Sir Thomas 115
novels 12, 58, 67, 121

O

Occam, William of 28, 69, 76, 106-107, 112
Occam's Razor 106, 131
Oedipus 39, 62
Orestes 39
Origen 77, 135, 137, 138, 139, 141, 147
Orphism 28, 52, 82, 91
Orwell, George, 15-16, 18, 24
Ostrogoths 96

Othello 39
Ovid 33
Oxford Calculators 107
Oxyrhynchus 94

P

Paglia, Camille 19
Painting 9, 53, 59, 60, 64, 110, 118, 124
Paladas 143-144
Palladianism 125
Pan 35
Paraclete 135, 138
Parthenon 60-61, 85
Pater, Walter 93, 117, 118, 123
Pavlov, Ivan 44
Pelikan, Jaroslav 137-138
Penrose, Roger 44-45
Pericles 81
Permissive Society 24-25
Petrarch 96, 109, 112-113, 125
Phaon 92
Pheidias 60, 85
Philo 118, 136
Pindar 33-34, 42
Pinker, Stephen 45
Plato: Academy 55, 90, 91: art 60, 61, 62: art as a copy 64, 115: on atheism 68, 70, 71, 73: Attic Greek 84: Beauty **59-60, 84-86**, 89, 90, 110, 111, 125, 126, 139, 144: Becoming 28, 40, 86, 90, 112, 126, 143: Being 29, 32, 40, 48, 58, 59-60, 62, 64, 65, 73, 90, 92, 112, 126, 129, 131,144: the Cave 88-89: Consciousness 28, 29, 35, 36, 37, 78, 79, 100, 104, 105, 109: Creator-God 139: Demiurge 76, 114: education 125: f5th century Enlightenment 49: falsification 83: The Forms (also Ideas, Eidoi) 53, 54, 62, 73, 85, **86-87**, 89, 97, 116: Forms as Abstractions **129-130**: Forms as

Realism/Nominalism 97-98: God and morals 77: The Good 76, 83, 89, 90, 138: The Good as God 76, 138: The Good and the Sun 89: The Good, The Truth and Beauty 62, 139: Gothic Architecture 110-111: Heavenly spheres 114, 116: and Hesychasm 108: holy philosophy 115, 127: on immateriality 81-82, 127: immortality, reasons for believing 82: inspiration 61-62: Kallipolis 64, 89: Magnesia 89: materialism 70: maths as way to Being 98: music 64-65: mysticism 87-88, 89, 90-91: Orphism – influence on 82: on pederasty 89-90: poetry 64, 65: pre-Christian Christian 140-14: pre-Plato Platonist - 33, 92, 139: Pythagoras – influence on 82: semi-Platonism 73: the Sun 88-89: Reincarnation - way to God is hard 138-139: self-fulfilment 24: Time 140: Wilde on Plato 124, 125, 126

Platonism: Augustinian Platonism 103, 104 139: Berkeley and Platonism 127, 129: Christianity and Platonism 139, 144-146: Gothic Cathedrals 110-111: Platonism explained **87, 144**, 91: Hermeticism 114: Hesychasm 108: Hypatia 143: *The Iliad* and Platonism 139: Dean Inge as Platonist 129: Leibnitz and 91: in Middle Ages 96, 115, 110-111, 113: morals 145: not collectivist 146: Platonism without knowing Plato 96: Personal Platonism 80: Petrarch 113: as a religion 144-146: Renaissance 113-116; and Shakespeare 114-

115: Scientific Revolution 114: Shelley as Platonist 21: spiritual exercises 90-91: Platonist spirituality 114: *The Tempest* as Platonist Vision 40:

Pletho 76, 113

Plotinus 28, 108: on Beauty 59-60: Beauty of colour 60: Beauty of a musical note 64-65: Beauty of Ideas 86-87: Beauty as way to Being 62: Beauty is inside the mind 36: and consciousness 36: cosmos as copy of what was in his mind 36: cut away crookedness in your mind 36: perfect goodness is inside the mind 36: earth as terrible place 142: house as Idea stamped on stone 86: love as response to Beauty 126: mystic 142: Renaissance 116: on self-loathing 15: his system 129-130. See also Neo-Platonism

Plutarch 52, 115, 145

Poetry 12, 21, 59, 60 et seq, **92-95**, 111, 112, 115, 120-121, 125, 126, 127, 143

Poets 19, 33, 41, 43, 49, 52, 61, 62, 65, 67, 92-95, 101, 121, 127, 143, 146

Political Correctness 23-24

Pope, Alexander 15, 51, 125, 132

Pope Clement IV 99

Pope John XXII 107

Pope John Paul II 75

Popper, Karl 83, 99

Porphyry 139, 142

Post-Modernism 27, 83

Post-Normal Science 27

Post-Structuralism 27

Pound, Ezra 63

Pre-Raphaelites 93

pre-Socratics 28, 35, 81, 82

Primrose League 71

Proclus 145-146
Prospero 40
Protagoras 68, 71
Psalm 14 69
Pseudo-Dionysius 96, 110 (see also St Denis)
Ptolemaic Cosmology 114
Pythagoras 28, 50, 82, 114, 138

Q
quale/qualia 47
Queen Anne 15, 51, 132
Queensberry, Marquis of 125-126
quiddity 102

R
Raphael 125
Ravetz, Jerome 27
Realism 28, 97, 101
Reformation 116, 136
Reincarnation 90,138-139
Relativism 28
Renaissance 28, 33, 41, 76, 93, 96, **112-116**, 117, 125
Renaissance (Medieval) 96, 97, 110
Renan, Ernest 147
Richard of St Victor 108
Riots, Alexandria 143
Robespierre, Maximilien de 20
Rolle, Richard 108
Romanticism 28
Rothko, Mark 60
Rousseau, Jacques **19-21**, 41
Ruskin, John 20, 59, 61, 62, 118, 123, 125
Ruysbroeck, John of 69, 88, 108

S
St Albert Magnus 103
St Anselm 48, 69, 98
St Augustine: Aquinas and 101, 104: consciousness 35-36: *crede ut intelligas* 69: evolution 139: Hellenised Christianity 139-
140: Just War 104: immaterial reality 140: knowledge of eternity through Grace 140: how we learn 101: collapse of Paganism 142-143: Petrarch, influence on 112-113: Platonic Forms 139: his Platonism 103, 104, 139: Platonism in the Middle Ages 96: St Albert Magnus, influence on 103: Time 240
St Bernard of Clairvaux 100
St Bernard of Citaux 111
St Bonaventura 108
St Denis 96, 108, 110, 111 (see also Pseudo-Dionysius)
St Francis 125
St John (4th Gospel) 135
St Justin Martyr 135, 138
St Luke (Gospel) 135, 136
St Mark (Gospel) 135
St Matthew (Gospel) 135, 136
St Paul 96, 135, 136, 137, 140
St Paul's Cathedral 125, 129
Salisbury, 3rd Marquess of 71
Sappho 33, 34, 50, 91, **92-95**
Scepticism 50. 70
Schelling, F W 70, 73
Scholasticism 109, 136
Schopenhauer, Arthur 51, 70
Schrödinger, Irwin 46
Scientific Revolution 11, 13, 41, 69, 99, 109, 114
Scottie (Star Trek) 46
Scotus, Duns 28, **101-12**
Scruton, Roger 12, 62-63
Secret Friends 69, 101
Seers 69
Seneca (Older and Younger) 55
Shaftesbury, 3rd Earl of 73
Shakespeare, William 11, 36, **37-40**, 41, 43, 47, 58, 67, 114-116
Schoenberg, Arnold 65
Siger of Brabant 69, 104
Shelley, Percy Bysshe 21, 31

Snell, Bruno **30-35**, 42-43, 134

Socialism 13, 16, 18, 26, 28, 79, 80, 104, 118, 119-121, 126, 132,

Socrates 51, 68: two strands of consciousness 24, 28: belief in absolute truth 83, 86: Anaxagoras 81-82: Beauty as way to the divine 84-85, 89, 90: explains cave myth 88-89: influence on Euripides 34: Euthyphro 92: dialectics 35, 83 et seq, 90: falsification 83: father 60: the Forms 86, 87,127: how important is human life? 90: knows nothing 83: monotheism 86, 76, 82: search for the Good 83: and Hippias 84-86: immateriality 81-82: immortality 82: inspiration 61-62: know thyself/unexamined life 34-35: Socratic Method 83-86, 101: invention of the soul 82: influenced by Orphism on 82: as pre-Christian martyr 138: prayer to Pan 35: influenced by Pythagoras on 82: Socratic Question, the 144: as Secret Friend 90: versus Sophists 63, 68, 73, 83

Sol Invicta 144

Sophists 63, 73, 82-83, 84

South Bank, London 65

Soviet Russia 13, 14, 16, 25, 77

Spengler, Oswald 9, 12, 39, 63,

State: city state 56, 68, 89, 92: Berkeley's ideal 132: Christianity as state religion 142: state gods 144: over-powerful 39: role of 54,104: socialist state 120, 121: Welfare State 20, 39, 79

Statism 12, 39

Statues – 36: Athena 60, 85: boy charioteer, 60-61: Chartres 111:

Heracles 143

Steele, Richard 70, 132

Stewart, J A 80

Stochhausen, Karlheinz 65

Stoicism 28, 50, **55-57**, 70, 76, 136, 138, 143, 144

Stravinsky, Igor 65

Strong, Maurice 26

substance 53, 98

Suger, Abbot 108, 110-111, 116

Surrealism 64

Suso 108

Swift, Jonathan 132

Swedenborg, Emanuel 118

Swinburne, Algernon 93

Swineshead, Richard 107

Sydney, Sir Philip 40, 114

Symeon 108

Symbolism 28, 59

T

terminism 106

Tertullian 53, 70, 138

Themis 34

Theodosius, Emperor 142

Theon 143

Thoreau, Henry David 25

Tocqueville, Alexis de 42

Titans, the 31

Tithonus 95

Tolkien, J R R 37

Trotskyism 75

Troubadours 111

U

Unmoved Mover 57

V

Vandals 96

Visigoths 96

Vlastos, Gregory 92

Voltaire, 70

W

Weber, Max 9-10

Welfarism 12, 20, 39, 79
Wells, H G 42
Whistler, J A M 124
Whitehead, Alfred North 62
Whitman, Walt 62
Wife of Bath 40
Wilde, Oscar 93: Aestheticism
  117-118: anti-journalist 121:
  anti-Middle Class 120-121:
  anti-Platonist phase 118: power
  of art 124: Beauty as Truth
  124: Bosie 122, 123, 125-126:
  Catholicism 125: Christian
  story, power of 146-147:
  culture as divine 123: death
  126: *Dorian Gray* synopsis 118-
  119: on education 125:
  epigrams 121-122: on landscape
  painting 124: Love 123:
  Michael Field 93: miracles 147:
music 124: mysticism 126: as a
  Platonist 116, 122, 125, 126:
  Reading Jail 122: on the
  Renaissance 125: as a
  revolutionary 121: self-
  destruction, fascination with
  126: socialism 119-121: in USA
  117-118
Woden 30
Wordsworth, William 41, 55, 78

X
Xenophanes 68

Y
Yates, Frances 113, 114

Z
Zeno (Stoic) 55
Zeus 30, 31, 34, 56, 76, 95